T0372752

OPEN WORLD

STRATEGY PLUS

B1
PRELIMINARY

INCLUSIVE
WORKBOOK

with Audio

Sheila Dignen

with Sarah Dymond and Jane Ritter

Cambridge University Press
www.cambridge.org/elt

Cambridge Assessment English
www.cambridgeenglish.org

Information on this title: www.cambridge.or/9781108464307

© Cambridge University Press and Cambridge Assessment 2021

First published 2021

20 19 18 17 16 15 14 13 12 11 10 9 8 7 6 5 4 3 2 1

Printed in Great Britain by CPI Group (UK) Ltd, Croydon CRO.4YY

A catalogue record for this publication is available from the British Library

ISBN 978-1-108-46430-7 Inclusive Workbook with Audio

CONTENTS

WELCOME TO OPEN WORLD

THE COURSE THAT TAKES YOU FURTHER

This workbook has the same aims and objectives as the original **Open World Workbook** in covering the course and preparing you for the exam. It is designed to give you further support both in the visual look and by giving additional help for exercises and tasks.

This workbook will also support you in thinking back to what you did in the Student's Book and will help you to look again at the language you learnt with clear links and other resources for the language covered.

It is important that you try the exercises first as this is the best way for you to learn. The support is there if you need it.

In Units Starter to 7 there are exercises and tasks with a lot of additional support for you. From Unit 8 to 14 you will notice you will have less support, though there will still be support with strategies, as well as resources that link with the Student's Book. The aim is to help you focus on your learning to take you to the next level and to encourage you to make your own decisions in your learning.

LEARN ABOUT THE FEATURES IN YOUR NEW INCLUSIVE WORKBOOK

CLEAR LINKS SHOW YOU WHERE TO FIND VOCABULARY Try the exercises first, then use the links to the Student's Book if you need more help.

GRAMMAR BOXES Use the short presentation boxes to remind you of the grammar from the Student's Book and the grammar animation.

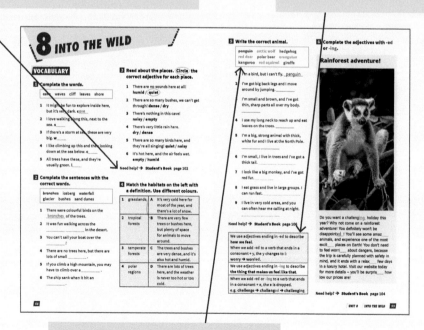

COLOUR CODING Helps you identify what to do in the task.

REMIND YOURSELF OF GRAMMAR STRUCTURES
Scan the purple QR codes and watch the short grammar animations as many times as you want.

CLEAR LINKS SHOW YOU WHERE TO FIND EXTRA GRAMMAR HELP
Try the exercises first, then use the links to the Grammar reference in the Student's Book if you need more help.

AUDIOSCRIPTS AT THE BACK OF THE BOOK
Scan the blue QR codes to listen to the task first, but if you want further help, use the audioscript to listen and read.

CLEAR LINKS SHOW YOU WHERE TO FIND MORE HELP WITH EXAM TASKS
Use the links to easily find more facts and tips about the Listening and Reading exam tasks.

HOW WAS UNIT ... ?
Think about the exercises in the unit and how much help you needed to do them.

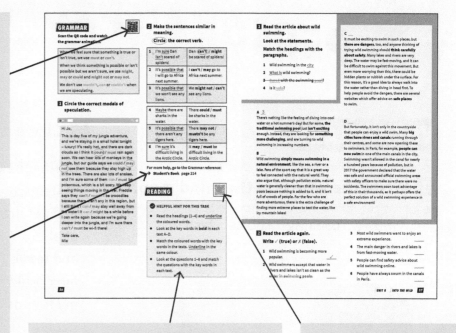

HELPFUL HINTS FOR THIS TASK
Read the hints and use colours to organise the task and help you complete it.

AUDIO OF READING TEXTS
Scan the orange QR codes and listen to an audio recording of the text.

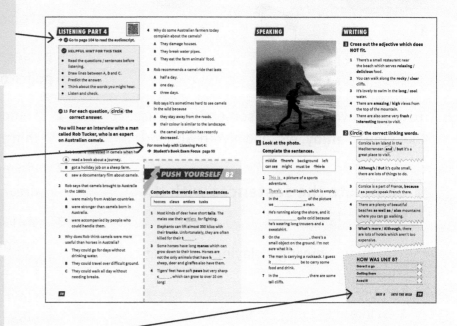

This final section is to support you in thinking about what you have learnt and also how you managed to complete the exercises and tasks. As well as making your choice between **Gave it a go**, **Getting there** and **Aced it!**, please think about why you made your choice from these three options. If you have not ticked **Aced it!** each time, think about what you did well, what you think you need to understand better, what further support you might need or what you can do yourself to get to **Aced it!** next time.

S PERSONAL PROFILE

VOCABULARY

1 **Write the words in the mind map.**

~~music~~ cooking sports fashion travel

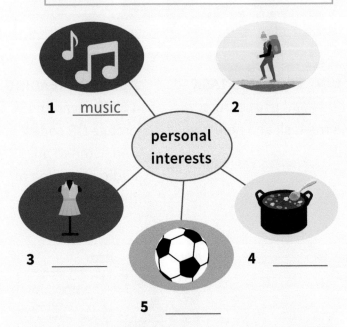

1 music
2 _____
3 _____
4 _____
5 _____

personal interests

To say how we feel about something we use: **like / love / enjoy**, etc. and a verb with **ing**.

2 **Complete the sentences with the verb + ing.**

learning buying playing cooking ~~listening~~

1 I like listening to **music**.

2 My brother enjoys _____ football and other **sports**.

3 Elsie loves _____ new **clothes**!

4 I enjoy _____ **meals** for my family.

5 I love _____ about different **fashions** in the past.

Need help? → **Student's Book** page 8

3 (Circle) the correct words.

During the week, I usually get (up) / **out** quite early, then I **have** / **make** a shower and get dressed. I **do** / **have** breakfast at about 7.30, and then I pick up my bag and **leave** / **go** to college. I have classes all morning, then I **take** / **have** lunch with my friends before the afternoon classes. I don't usually meet **up** / **to** with my friends in the evenings, because I have a part-time job as a waiter. When I'm not working, I like keeping fit, so I often work **out** / **off** at the gym.

4 **Complete the words in the sentences.**

gardener architect journalist police officer ~~sales assistant~~ chef

1 I enjoy **helping customers** choose things to **buy**. I'm a s ales a ssistant .

2 I love **food** and **cooking**, so this is my dream job! I'm a c_____ .

3 My job helps people know **what's happening** in the **world**. I'm a j_____ .

4 I love working **outside**. I'm happy when I see my **plants** growing. I'm a g_____ .

5 I am happy when people move into a new **house** that I've **designed**. I'm an a_____ .

6 I help **reduce crime**. I'm a p_____ o_____ .

Need help? → **Student's Book** pages 9 and 11

GRAMMAR

Scan the QR codes and watch the grammar animations.

	present simple	present continuous
Positive (+):	They <u>usually</u> take lots of photos. The lake **freezes** <u>every</u> winter.	I'm working <u>at the moment</u>. He's making pasta <u>today</u>.
Negative (–):	Claudia **doesn't come** from Milan. You **don't speak** German.	Jack's **not listening** to music <u>now</u>. They're **not playing** football <u>this week</u>.
Questions (?):	**Do** you **run** to work <u>most</u> days? Where **does** Ben **work** <u>at the weekend</u>?	What **is** Laura **doing** <u>now</u>? Why **are** you <u>always</u> **taking** my bike without asking?
words used with:	**Adverbs of frequency: always, usually, sometimes.** These come before the verb. **Expressions of frequency: every** (day), **once a** (week), **on** (Fridays), **most** (nights). These are used at the beginning or the end of sentences.	**at the moment** **now** **this** (week, month) **today**
use to talk:	about habits. about things that are generally or always true.	about a temporary activity. about things that are happening now. about annoying habits with <u>always</u>.

1 Complete the sentences with the correct present simple or present continuous form of the verbs.

1 He never **(get up)** <u>gets up</u> early!

2 Mmm, I **(enjoy)** _____ this soup – it's lovely!

3 Architects usually **(earn)** _____ a lot of money.

4 My sister **(borrow)** _____ always _____ my clothes without asking. It's so annoying!

5 More people **(become)** _____ vegetarians now.

2 Match the halves of the sentences. Use different colours.

1 **What** are	A does the film **start**?
2 **What time**	B **going** home now?
3 **Are** they	C you **doing**?

4 **Does** Sam **work**	D Max talking **to**?
5 **Who** is	E have for **breakfast**?
6 **What** do you **usually**	F in a **restaurant** as a chef?

3 Write the question words and your own answers.

> Why   When   ~~Where~~   How
> What   Who

1 A: <u>Where</u> do you **live**?

   B: I live in _____ .

2 A: _____ do you **hang out with**
      at the weekend?

   B: With my _____ .

3 A: _____ are your **exams**?

   B: They're _____ .

4 A: _____ **old** are you?

   B: I'm _____ .

5 A: _____ do you **do** on
      Saturdays?

   B: I often _____ .

6 A: _____ are you **happy** today?

   B: Because _____ .

4 Complete the posts with the correct present simple or present continuous form of the verbs.

🔍 🏠

What do you love and hate about Mondays?

JayT44 At the moment I **(study)** <u>'m studying</u>
to be an architect. Mondays are difficult for me
because I **(be)** _____ usually tired after
the weekend!

EllieZZ I sometimes **(go)** _____ away
with friends for the weekend. It's great, except
my friend Anna **(borrow)** _____ always
_____ my clothes and make-up!

Joe99 On Mondays I **(have)** _____
a really difficult maths class. I have to study
maths because I **(train)** _____ to be a
mechanic, but I **(hate)** _____ it!

For more help, go to the Grammar reference:
→ **Student's Book** pages 196–198

READING

🔘 **HELPFUL HINT FOR THIS TASK**

● Read the question and <u>underline</u> the
  key words.

● Look at the key words in **bold** in each
  text 1–6.

● Look at the questions A–F and match
  the questions with the key words
  in each text. <u>Underline</u> in the same
  colour.

1 Read an interview with Tom who is a ninja in Japan.

Match the questions A–F with the texts 1–6.

A Is it difficult to become a ninja?

B ~~What is a ninja?~~

C Is there anything you don't like
   about the job?

D What's your daily routine like?

E What do you enjoy the most about
   your job?

F What does a professional ninja do
   nowadays?

1 B

Ninjas are traditional fighters in Japan. They usually fight using their hands. They also use high jumps and kicks, so they're very fit. There aren't any real ninjas now, but people still learn the skills because ninjas are important in Japanese culture.

2

Some towns and cities in Japan employ ninjas because tourists like them. The ninjas put on shows of their skills in the streets. They also talk to tourists about the ninja traditions. Tourists also love taking photos of themselves with a ninja!

3

Yes, it is. You have to be very fit, and you have to practise a lot to learn all the skills. You also need a good memory, because you need to learn about the history of ninjas and why they're important in Japanese culture.

4

I get up early and have a light breakfast. Then I practise my skills for two hours. I often practise with other ninjas, which is fun. Then at 10.30 I start work in the city centre. We do four or five shows a day, so it's quite tiring. Then in the evenings I usually work out for an hour, because you need to be strong to be a ninja. So there isn't much time for hanging out with friends!

5

Everything! I really like learning the ninja skills. You feel so good when you manage to do something new. At the moment I'm trying to learn a really difficult move, and I love that challenge. I also enjoy talking to the tourists, especially the kids. They're funny because they always want to fight me!

6

Yes, I hate the fact that I can't have chips or chocolate! Ninjas have to be small and not very heavy, so I'm very careful about what I eat. But it's worth it so I can do a job that I love.

2 **Read again. Write ✓ (true) or ✗ (false).**

1 There are still a few real ninjas in Japan.　　　　　　　　✗

2 Modern ninjas work to entertain tourists.　　　　　　　　_____

3 You have to learn skills and study to become a ninja.　　_____

4 Tom spends a lot of time relaxing with friends.　　　　_____

5 Tom finds children annoying when he's working.　　　　_____

6 Tom can't eat all the things he would like to eat.　　　　_____

3 **Look at the words in yellow in the text. Match them with the meanings 1–5.**

traditional ~~employ~~ culture light challenge

1 give someone a job　　　　　employ

2 with not much food　　　　　_____

3 belonging to the past and the culture of a country　　_____

4 something that is difficult to do or learn　　　　　_____

5 the way of life and beliefs that the people of a country share　_____

LISTENING

→ 🎧 Go to page 96 to read the audioscript.

1 🎧 02 **Listen to people talking about their jobs and routines.**

(Circle) **the job that each person does or wants to do.**

1   Maria   **restaurant chef /** ⟨**cookery vlogger**⟩

2   Sam   **teacher / tennis player**

3   Anika   **journalist / doctor**

✓ **HELPFUL HINT FOR THIS TASK**

● <u>Underline</u> the key words in each sentence.

● Think about what words the speaker might use instead of these words.

---

2 🎧 02 **Listen again. Write ✓ (true) or ✗ (false).**

1   Maria <u>doesn't want</u> to <u>work</u> **in the evenings**.   ✓
    Maria might say 'don't like writing at night'.

2   Maria **isn't making money**.   _____

3   Sam **is winning competitions**.   _____

4   Sam **often** eats out.   _____

5   Anika **is working** and **also** studying.   _____

6   Anika meets **different people** as part of her job.   _____

---

3 🎧 03 **Complete the sentences with the correct words. Then listen and check.**

~~in~~	at	for	for	to	as

1   I'm really interested __in__ **food**.

2   I don't want to work _____ **a chef** in a restaurant.

3   I'm winning quite a lot of games _____ **the moment**.

4   I also listen _____ **music** a lot at home.

5   I also **work** _____ a newspaper in my town.

6   This is the right job _____ **me**.

SPEAKING

1 Read the questions and (circle) the correct response.

1 A: What's your name?
   B: (It's Paul.) / He's Paul.

2 A: Nice to meet you!
   B: I'm 20. / Nice to meet you too!

3 A: Where are you from?
   B: New York. / No, I don't.

4 A: What do you do?
   B: I love reading books. / I'm a journalist.

5 A: How are you?
   B: I'm American. / I'm fine, thanks.

2 (Circle) the correct response.

1 A: I go running three times a week.
   B: I agree. I like running, too. / (Really? I like running, too.)

2 A: Hi. My name's George.
   B: Nice to meet you. / How are you?

3 A: I love cooking.
   B: I am too. / Me too.

4 A: I'm an architect.
   B: That sounds interesting. / I agree. Do you design new houses?

5 A: I think the job of a police officer is very difficult.
   B: Really? And it's dangerous, too. / I agree. It's quite dangerous, too.

6 A: I work in London.
   B: Really? What do you do? / That sounds interesting. How are you?

WRITING

1 Complete the blog entry with the correct words.

> ~~name's~~ eight town cooking food
> computer programmer blog

Hello! My ___name's___ Alejandro and I'm 22. I'm Spanish and I live in Madrid. **I'm a** _____ and I work for a big computer company. Welcome to my _____ !

I **usually** get up at seven o'clock and I **start work at** _____ . I get home at about seven in the evening and I prepare **some** _____ . Then I **usually** watch TV before I go to bed.

I love sport, especially football. I **play for a team in my** _____ and I also love watching sport on TV. I also **enjoy** _____ . I can make really good pizzas!

2 (Circle) the correct words.

Hello! My name's Rob and I'm (18 years old) / 18 year old. At the moment **I'm study / I'm studying** to become a police officer. Welcome to my blog!

My classes **start usually / usually start** at nine o'clock, so I always get up early. I **always am / am always** tired when I get home in the evenings. At the weekend, I **enjoy hanging / enjoy hang** out with my friends, and we often go to the cinema together.

HOW WAS THE STARTER UNIT?

Gave it a go ⌐⌐

Getting there ⌐⌐

Aced it! ⌐⌐

1 GETTING AWAY

VOCABULARY

1 Match the halves of the sentences. Use different colours.

1	I always feel excited when I'm **packing**	A	many **souvenirs** to take home with me.
2	I love **discovering**	B	my **bags** to go on holiday.
3	I don't **buy**	C	**new places** when I'm on holiday.

4	I always **take**	D	in the **mountains**.
5	I like **hiking**	E	**games** on the beach with friends.
6	I always have fun **playing**	F	lots of **photos**!

Need help? ➔ **Student's Book** page 14

2 Complete the sentences. Write the letters.

1 I think going on a **long** A **by train** would be really boring!
   A journey   B travel

2 We're going on **a ten-day __** to Morocco next month.
   A trip   B travel

3 **Flying** is not always the most expensive **form of __**.
   A transport   B trip

4 We went on a **__ of the** old city.
   A journey   B tour

5 I'd love to do a job that involves **a lot of __**.
   A travel   B journey

Need help? ➔ **Student's Book** page 17

3 Complete the sentences with the correct weather words.

~~cool~~ climate mild dull lightning damp

1 It's quite **c**ool__ today, so you might need a sweatshirt.

2 I hate it when the weather's **grey and d**_____ .

3 What's the **c**_____ like where you live?

4 I hate it when it rains and everything feels **d**_____ .

5 There was a storm last night, with lots of thunder and **l**_____ .

6 I don't like cold weather, so I'd prefer to live in a place where the weather's **m**_____ .

4 Circle the correct words.

JJ44   I'm looking for somewhere to go on a hiking holiday in November. Any suggestions?

Marty_P   The island of Madeira is nice at that time of year. It's quite warm, with blue skies and plenty of (sunshine) / climate. It's a nice dry heat, too, so it doesn't feel too **dull / humid**. Perfect!

SammyT33   I went to the Caribbean last year, but I wouldn't recommend it in November. It's the beginning of the wet season, so there may be frequent heavy **chilly / showers** and a strong **breeze / dull**.

Suzy_S21   Why not go to Tenerife? It doesn't often rain there, so you can be fairly sure you'll get **fine / dull** weather. Nights can be **mild / chilly**, though, so take a few warmer clothes with you.

Need help? ➔ **Student's Book** page 19

GRAMMAR

a   b

Scan the QR codes and watch the grammar animations.

1 Complete the advice.

Use comparatives or superlatives.

Booking a holiday

Price isn't everything when you're booking a holiday, and the **(cheap)** cheapest holiday isn't necessarily the **(good)** _____ one. One hotel may cost less than another, but it may be a distance from the airport, so it's **(expensive)** _____ to get there by taxi. Also, a hotel that has low prices might have a **(small)** _____ pool than other hotels. This probably means the pool will be **(crowded)** _____ and not much fun! Many people choose a big hotel because they think this will have the **(comfortable)** _____ rooms. But this isn't always true.

2 Circle the correct words so the sentence has a similar meaning.

The highlighted words will help.

1 This hotel is older than that one.
   That hotel **(isn't as old)** / **is less old** as this one.

2 The beach was more crowded yesterday than it is today.
   The beach is **less crowded** / **isn't as crowded** today than it was yesterday.

3 This restaurant is less expensive than the Italian one.
   This restaurant **is less expensive** / **isn't as expensive** as the Italian one.

4 This beach is beautiful, and the one we went to yesterday was beautiful too.
   This beach is as **beautiful as** / **less beautiful** the one we went to yesterday.

3 Circle the correct words.

1 The pool was **(too)** / **enough** cold to swim in!

2 There were lots of restaurants, but they were all **too** / **enough** expensive for us.

3 Our balcony wasn't big **too** / **enough** for us to sit on.

4 We only stayed for a few days, so we didn't have **too** / **enough** time to do very much.

4 Circle the correct words.

1 I'm **(so)** / **such a** happy that I'm going on holiday tomorrow!

2 Why have you got **so** / **such a** big bag?

3 Spain is **so** / **such a** lovely country to visit!

4 It was **so** / **such a** exciting going on the boat trip.

5 Circle the correct words.

I'm having **so** / **(such)** a great time here in Ireland. The countryside is even **more** / **the most** beautiful than I expected, and the people here are **enough** / **so** friendly and welcoming.

The **more** / **most** surprising thing is the food – it's amazing, and it's **less** / **as** expensive than I thought, which is good!

The **too big** / **biggest** problem has been travelling around. The buses here are **cheaper** / **so cheap** than the trains, but there aren't many of them in the countryside.

For more help, go to the Grammar reference:
→ **Student's Book** pages 199–201

LISTENING

→ 🎧 Go to page 96 to read the audioscript.

1 🎧 **04 Listen to an interview on a holiday show. What is the show about?**

A an unusual holiday on a cruise ship that costs a lot of money

B a holiday company that wants to pay someone to go on holiday

2 🎧 **04 Listen again. Write ✓ (true) or ✗ (false).**

1 The company wants someone to go on seven different holidays.   ___✗___

2 The person has to write a blog and upload photos to social media.   _____

3 The person also has to upload a video, but they can't choose what it is about.   _____

4 The company is employing this person to help advertise its holidays.   _____

5 To apply, you should write to the company and send some of your holiday photos.   _____

READING PART 2

> **❗ HELPFUL HINT FOR THIS TASK**
>
> - Read the question and underline the key words.
> - Colour the border of each photograph.
> - Use a different colour for each photo.
> - Underline the name and key words in each text that relate to the hotel they want.
> - Find similar words in the hotel descriptions.

For each question, choose the correct answer.

The people below all want to find a hotel near the beach.

On page 15 there are eight hotels near the beach.

Decide which hotel would be most suitable for the people below.

1
Tanya wants a hotel directly on the beach so she can go for long walks. Apart from that, she doesn't plan to leave her hotel so wants all meals and plenty of things to do there.

G

2
Susie wants to stay at a small quiet hotel. She wants the hotel to provide transport to a nearby town so that she can do lots of shopping there.

3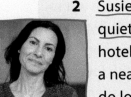
Rafael needs a hotel which provides suitable activities and food for young children. He also wants the hotel restaurant to serve a range of international food that he and his wife can enjoy.

___

4
Tommy is looking for a hotel with access to a gym and swimming pool. He also wants his hotel to be within walking distance of entertainment facilities for the evenings.

___

5
Angelica and her sister Katrin want a hotel which is next to a busy beach where they can take lessons in a watersport and go swimming in the sea.

___

HOLIDAY HOTELS

A Dunes Hotel

You never need to step outside this hotel as it has a full programme of activities for adults, from fitness classes and yoga to cooking lessons and garden tours. There's also a choice of four restaurants to suit different tastes. The balcony has fantastic views over the town and the beach beyond.

B Ocean View

It's easy to visit the local attractions – a castle and a children's fun park – because the public bus stops outside the hotel entrance. Behind the hotel is a small beach which is often crowded with sunbathers and swimmers. There's also a diving and sailing school, where hotel guests can get a discount.

C Seaside Hotel

This small, family-owned hotel offers fantastic home-cooked food. The hotel is only five minutes' walk to a busy beach but it's outside a town. If guests wish to go out in the evenings, it's better to bring your own car or hire one.

D Golden Sands Hotel

This friendly hotel has a fantastic sports and entertainment programme to keep kids busy all day. There's only one restaurant but the menu changes daily, includes food from around the world and is suitable for all ages. There's an evening babysitting service so that adults can eat later.

E International Hotel

This busy hotel is ten minutes on foot to the town where there are discos and nightly concerts. The fitness centre's great for those who want to stay active on holiday, and guests can use the twenty-five-metre pool at the hotel next door. Free transport is provided to and from the airport.

F Harry's Hotel

This hotel is right on the beach so guests can sit and watch surfers in the water. There are only twenty-five bedrooms so the atmosphere's always peaceful. All meals are provided and are cooked by a French chef. The town centre's great for buying gifts, clothes and shoes, and the hotel minibus takes guests there for free.

G Luxus Hotel

This hotel, located away from the town, has everything you need, from a large swimming pool, games room and gym to clothes shops and a mini-supermarket. Breakfast and dinner are included, and it's possible to add lunch for a small charge. To reach the five-kilometre sandy beach, guests just need to cross the hotel garden.

H Sunset Hotel

A ten-minute taxi ride along the coast takes guests to a nearby town with a choice of watersports, including surfing and windsurfing lessons, as well as lively nightlife. The hotel has a private beach for sunbathing, but for swimming it's best to use the hotel pool.

For more help with Reading Part 2:
→ **Student's Book Exam Focus** page 22

SPEAKING

1 Complete the words in the sentences.

> think   agree   right   ~~Perhaps~~
> true   agree   Really   think

suggestion	**P**erhaps they could visit a museum. I **t**_____ they should go to the beach.
asking for opinion	Do you **a**_____ ? What do you **t**_____ ?
agreeing	Yes, you're **r**_____ . That's **t**_____ .
disagreeing	Sorry, but I don't **a**_____ . **R**_____ ?

2 Complete the words in the conversations.

> ~~think~~   great   afraid   enjoy
> ~~might~~   best

1 A: They **m**ight like a trip to the theatre.
   B: Do you **t**hink so? I'm not sure.

2 A: I think the **b**_____ way to get to Paris is by train.
   B: I'm **a**_____ I disagree with you. The train is too slow.

3 A: I think they'd **e**_____ going shopping.
   B: I think that's a **g**_____ idea. Most people like shopping.

3 Circle the correct phrases.

1 A: Perhaps **they could** / they might like spend the day sightseeing.
   B: That's true. / Really? I think that might be fun.

2 A: I think they'd enjoy / I think they should visiting the zoo.
   B: Do you agree? / Yes, you're right. They'd like that.

3 A: I think a barbecue is the best idea for a meal. **What do you think?** / Really?
   B: I'm afraid I disagree with you. / Yes, you're right. A barbecue isn't fun if it's raining.

4 Circle the best answer to each question.

1 A: Do you prefer to travel by plane or by train?
   B: **I'd rather go by plane because it's quicker.** / Trains are usually a bit cheaper.

2 A: What do you think of organised tours?
   B: I sometimes go on organised tours. / I think organised tours can be interesting sometimes.

3 A: Would you rather spend a day sunbathing or sightseeing?
   B: I love sunbathing. / I'd prefer to go sightseeing for the day.

4 A: What's the best time of year for you to go on holiday?
   B: Spring is my favourite time to go on holiday. / The summer is usually too expensive for some people.

Complete the words in the sentences.

> fossil fuels environmentally friendly
> waste conservation carbon footprint
> ~~climate change~~

1 Some parts of the world are getting much warmer because of **c**limate **c**hange .

2 Plastic water bottles are definitely not **e**_____ **f**_____!

3 Travelling by train rather than plane will reduce your **c**_____ **f**_____ .

4 We all need to recycle more so that we produce less **w**_____ .

5 We should use clean forms of energy rather than burning **f**_____ **f**_____ .

6 It's important to support the **c**_____ of the rainforest.

WRITING

1 Circle the correct linking words.

1 **Although** / **But** the beach was crowded, there was enough space for us to find a place to relax.

2 The city centre has some beautiful old buildings. **What's more / As well**, there are also some amazing shops.

3 **As well as / Also** visiting the museum, we also had time for lunch in a small café.

4 The food was excellent, **and / but** the waiters were all very friendly.

5 The hotel has two swimming pools, and tennis courts **also / too**.

2 Complete the sentences with the correct linking words.

> also too As well as Although
> though ~~and~~

1 A helicopter trip is a **great way to see** the city, _and_ it **doesn't cost** too **much**.

2 The old city centre is lovely, and the castle is _____ **worth** a visit.

3 _____ we were **tired**, we **decided to go** for a walk along the beach.

4 _____ _____ _____ **being** very crowded, the museum was old-fashioned and not very interesting.

5 The park is a **great place** to relax. There's a very **good café** there, _____ .

6 We had an **amazing holiday**. It was very **expensive**, _____ .

HOW WAS UNIT 1?

Gave it a go ☐

Getting there ☐

Aced it! ☐

2 ENTERTAIN ME

VOCABULARY

1 Write the words for entertainment.

> ~~soundtrack~~ thriller comedy
> episode audience

1 The **music** that plays during a **film.**
   s<u>oundtrack</u>

2 The **people** who watch a **play. a**_____

3 A very **exciting film** or **book. t**_____

4 **One part** of a **TV series. e**_____

5 A **film** that makes you laugh. **c**_____

Need help? → **Student's Book** page 28

GRAMMAR

Scan the QR code and watch the grammar animation.

past simple	present perfect
to talk about things that happened at a **definite time** in the past. We often use it with words like **ago, last** and **yesterday.**	to talk about **experiences** that have happened **some time up to now.** We often use it with **ever, never, already** and **yet.**
positive (+) I **visited** Rome two years <u>ago.</u>	positive (+) I've **visited** Rome <u>three times.</u>
Negative (-) We **didn't see** the film <u>last</u> weekend.	Negative (-) We've <u>never</u> seen that film.
Questions (?) **Did** he **leave** school <u>in 2019?</u>	Questions (?) **Have** they <u>ever</u> been to New York?

1 Complete the text with the correct **past simple** or **present perfect** form of the verbs.

Nearly a star!

I **(be)** <u>'ve</u> **never** <u>been</u> interested in being on TV, but **last year** a friend of mine **(go)** _____ to an event to find good singers for a talent show. He **always (love)** _____ singing. He **(sing)** _____ well for the judges. They **(accept)** _____ him onto the show. He's really excited because he **(not do)** _____ anything like this before.

2 Complete the questions with the correct **past simple** or **present perfect** form of the verbs.

1 **(you / enjoy)** <u>Did you enjoy</u> the concert **last Saturday**?

2 **(Paul / see)** _____ the new Star Wars film **yet**?

3 **(you / go)** _____ to any festivals **last summer**?

4 **(your friends / organise)** _____ **ever** _____ a surprise party for you?

5 **(Freya / win)** _____ the singing competition **last week**?

6 **(you / act)** _____ **ever** _____ in a play?

We use the **present perfect** to talk about things that started in the past and are still true now.

We use since with the **present perfect** and a point in time.

We use for with the **present perfect** and a period of time.

3 ⬭Circle⬭ the correct words.

1 I've been at this college **for / (since)** 2019.

2 Ollie has worked at the café **for / since** three months.

3 My brother has had this tablet **for / since** last year.

4 I've known Laura **for / since** five years.

5 Hana has been interested in dance **for / since** she was five.

6 My grandparents have lived in this house **for / since** a long time.

We use **already** when we have done something.	We use **yet** when we haven't done something but we plan to do it.
Martin has **already** left. They have **already** sold all the tickets.	We also use **yet** in questions. Has Dale called **yet**? The show hasn't started **yet**.
Already is placed between have / has and the past participle.	**Yet** is placed at the end of the sentence.

4 Complete the conversation with already and yet.

A: Have you seen the series Secret Lives _yet_ ?

B: No, I haven't. I haven't had time to watch it _____ . But I've _____ decided that it was David who killed Magda.

A: Really? I think there are a few possibilities.

B: Yes, but the police have _____ found things that show it's David.

A: Hmm, but they haven't arrested him _____ , so I'm not sure.

We use **used to** + **verb** for talking about things that were true in the past but are not true now.

To make **negative sentences** or **questions** with used to, we use **did / didn't + use to**. The verb that follows is always in the infinitive form.

5 ⬭Circle⬭ the correct form of used to.

In the early days of film-making, things use to / ⬭used to⬭ be very different for the actors. Firstly, they didn't use to / didn't used to **speak** in the films, because there was no sound. Someone use to / used to **play** the piano in cinemas while the audience watched the film. And how did they use to / used to **do** dangerous things? Nowadays, film makers can use computers to make things look exciting, or they use special actors to do the dangerous scenes. But in the 1920s that didn't use to / didn't used to **happen**. The main actors use to / used to **perform** in every scene, even when it was dangerous!

For more help, go to the Grammar reference:
→ **Student's Book** pages 202–203

LISTENING PART 2

→ **Go to page 97 to read the audioscript.**

> ❗ **HELPFUL HINT FOR THIS TASK**
>
> - Read each question and underline the key words.
> - Draw lines between A, B and C.
> - Listen carefully and use the script if necessary.

🎧 05 **For each question, ⟨circle⟩ the correct answer.**

1 You will hear two friends talking about a film they've just seen.

   What does the woman say?
   A The film was too long.
   Ⓑ The story was hard to follow.
   C The main actor was disappointing.

2 You will hear a brother and sister talking about booking concert tickets.

   They agree to book seats
   A near the stage.
   B at the side.
   C in the balcony.

3 You will hear a woman telling a friend about a TV programme.

   What type of programme did she watch?
   A a soap opera
   B a crime series
   C a documentary

4 You will hear two people talking about online newspapers.

   Why does the man prefer online newspapers to TV news?
   A They're more suitable for his busy lifestyle.
   B They focus on more interesting topics.
   C They provide more detailed information.

5 You will hear a man telling a friend about a play called The Visit.

   How does he feel?
   A satisfied that he's seen it
   B impressed by the way that it ended
   C excited about the director's next play

6 You will hear two friends talking about a summer music festival.

   One thing the woman likes about the festival is that
   A it isn't too crowded.
   B tickets aren't too expensive.
   C travelling there isn't too difficult.

For more help with Listening Part 2:
→ **Student's Book Exam Focus** page 34

READING

! HELPFUL HINT FOR THIS TASK

- Read the question and underline the key words.
- Look at the highlighted words in the questions and the paragraphs.
- Underline the key words in each paragraph that relate to the options in the questions.

1 Read the article. Choose A or B to answer the question below.

A Superhero films are popular now. The use of computers has made superhero films better.

B Film makers now use better stories in superhero films, so they are more exciting.

2 Read again. Circle the correct words.

1 Most of the **characters** in superhero films **have changed / haven't changed** since the 1960s. (paragraph 1)

2 Most people **can imagine they are / wouldn't like to be** a **superhero**. (paragraph 2)

3 **Audiences** thought the first superhero films **were amazing / looked disappointing**. (paragraph 3)

4 Superhero films are better now because **they look more like the stories in comics / they look more realistic** on **screen**. (paragraph 4)

5 Computers and **special effects** help **young people / people of all ages** enjoy superhero films. (paragraph 6)

Why do we suddenly love superheroes?

1 Everyone is suddenly crazy about superhero films! But why? Most of the **characters** are **not new**. They have been in stories in comics since the 1960s. So why are superhero films suddenly so popular now?

2 One reason is that the basic superhero story is very simple and familiar. **We would all love to be a superhero** — a normal person who gets amazing magic powers. We then use these powers to fight a bad guy who wants to destroy the world, and everyone loves us! Wonderful!

3 These stories worked well in **comics**. But with superhero films in the past, **this didn't work**. The **audience couldn't believe** the story they were watching. They could see that the superheroes weren't really flying, or climbing up walls. They just looked like normal people in rather silly clothes!

4 This has all changed. Budgets are much bigger and films are much better than they used to be. The **costumes** actors wear now are amazing. Film makers now use computers to make the superheroes look real. **When we see Superman flying, we can now believe that he is flying on screen.**

5 Because the stories now look real on the **screen**, we can enjoy them again. We can believe there really is a superhero, and he (or she) really can save the world! At the same time, we can enjoy the amazing pictures, the **soundtrack** and the excellent acting.

6 Fans have waited for a long time to see good superhero films. With the help of computers and amazing **special effects**, **everyone can really enjoy these simple stories of magic and power**, and good defeating bad.

Circle the correct phrasal verbs.

1	I used to be good friends with Ali, but I _fell out_ with him last year.	(fell out) / chilled out
2	My brother has really _____ tennis recently – he loves it!	got into / turned down
3	You shouldn't worry about things so much – you should _____ more!	keep on / chill out
4	Henry was really upset when his band _____ last year.	split up / let down
5	I think if you enjoy acting, you should _____ doing it – don't listen to anyone else!	turn down / keep on
6	My parents always want me to do well, and I don't want to _____.	let them down / get into them

SPEAKING

1 **Complete the words in the conversations.**

crazy	thing	~~stand~~	into	fan	mind

1 **A:** We could watch a film on your phone.

  B: No. I can't s**tand** watching films on my phone – the screen's far too small!

2 **A:** Do you want to go bowling later?

  B: No, I don't like bowling – it isn't my t_____.

3 **A:** Did you enjoy that film?

  B: Yes. I'm not usually a f_____ of romantic films, but this one was quite good.

4 **A:** Does your sister like that new band, New Day?

  B: Yes, they're her favourite band now. She's completely c_____ about them!

5 **A:** Have you heard the new song by Tamara?

  B: Yes, it's great. I'm really i_____ her music.

6 **A:** Where do you want to sit?

  B: Well, I don't m_____ sitting near the back of the cinema, but I'd prefer to be nearer the front.

WRITING

1 **Look at the sentences for informal emails. Are they beginnings or endings? Write.**

_____	_____
Hi,	Bye for now.
Hi Anna,	See you soon.
Dear Anna,	I'm looking forward to seeing you.

2 **Circle the correct form for informal emails.**

1 **There is / There's** a concert next Saturday.

2 **Where's / Where is** the festival taking place?

3 **I will / I'll** get the tickets.

4 **I'd love / I would love** to come with you.

5 **That is / That's** a really nice idea.

6 **Jack is coming / Jack's coming** to the concert with us.

3 **Circle the correct words.**

Hi Lucas,

Would / Do you like to come for a pizza with me and some friends tonight? We **could / may** meet in town, if you like.

Hope you can come!

Sam

Hi Sam,

Thanks for the invitation. **Sorry, but / No, but** I have to revise tonight because I've got exams tomorrow. How about **go / going** tomorrow night instead?

Bye for now,

Lucas

Hi Lucas,

That sounds / That's a nice idea. Let's **meet / meeting** at seven o'clock. Why **we don't / don't we** ask Kallum to come too?

Looking forward to seeing you,

Sam

4 **Look at the sentences. Are they suggestions, invitations or responses? Write.**

_____	_____	_____
Would you like...	Why don't we...	That's a nice idea!
How about verb + ing...	Let's meet...	Sorry, but...
	We could...	

For more help with Writing Part 1:
→ **Student's Book** page 227

HOW WAS UNIT 2?

Gave it a go ☐

Getting there ☐

Aced it! ☐

3 DINING OUT, EATING IN

VOCABULARY

1 Complete the text with the words.

> ~~meal~~ starter course bill bowl
> dish tip

I had a <u>meal</u> in an Italian restaurant last night, with some friends. I had a _____ of really nice soup first, as a _____ . I couldn't decide which _____ to have for my main _____ . In the end I had fish. It was nice, but I couldn't finish it all. I did manage some ice cream for dessert, though! When the _____ came, I was surprised because it wasn't too expensive. We left a big _____ for the waiter, because he was really helpful.

2 Circle the correct words.

You should definitely try this restaurant. It _serves_ really good food!	gives / **serves**
The waiter was friendly when he _____ us to our table.	asked / showed
It was a bit slow. We waited quite a long time for the waiter to _____ us the menu.	carry / bring
Very helpful waitress. She _____ our coats and helped us choose what to eat.	lifted / took
We _____ our food at 7.30 and didn't eat until 8.30!	ordered / demanded
Excellent food, but you need to _____ a table before you go.	keep / reserve

Need help? ➔ **Student's Book** page 41

3 Circle the correct words. These words will help you.

Pasta with mushroom sauce

(Chop) / **Put** some onions and garlic into **small pieces**, and **pour** / **slice** the mushrooms.

Fry / **Boil** these for a few minutes in a large pan with some **oil**.

Add / **Mix** salt and pepper **and** some fresh herbs, **and** a little cream.

Heat / **Slice** gently for a few minutes.

Meanwhile, **boil** / **fry** some pasta **in water**.

To serve, **put** / **slice** the pasta onto **the plate** and pour the mushroom sauce over the pasta.

Need help? ➔ **Student's Book** page 46

GRAMMAR

> quite / fairly / really / very / extremely +
> **neutral or mild** adjectives
> e.g. It looks good. ~~It's absolutely good.~~
> really / absolutely + **strong** adjectives.
> e.g. It tastes absolutely delicious. ~~It's extremely delicious.~~

1 Underline the correct modifiers.

1 Mmm, this soup tastes **very** / <u>absolutely</u> delicious!

2 Those biscuits look **quite** / absolutely nice.

3 That fish smells **really** / absolutely good.

4 Those desserts look **extremely** / absolutely gorgeous!

2 Complete the sentences. Write the letters.

1 Shall I add **a** <u>B</u> **salt** to the soup?
   A few   **B** little

2 There **isn't** ___ **ice cream** in the freezer.
   A any   **B** some

3 There **are a** ___ **biscuit<u>s</u>** left.
   A few   **B** little

4 There **isn't** ___ **milk** in the fridge.
   A many   **B** much

5 There **are** ___ **onion<u>s</u>** in this recipe.
   A no   **B** any

3 Complete the conversation with the correct words.

little   few   ~~many~~   any   much   some

A: How <u>many</u> apples do we need?

B: We only need a _____ – just two or three, I think.

A: Would you like _____ coffee?

B: No thanks. I don't drink _____ coffee – just one cup in the morning.

A: I'm thirsty. Is there _____ apple juice?

B: No, but there's a _____ orange juice.

4 Circle the correct words.

1 We only have **a few** / **many** eggs.

2 There isn't **some** / **any** cake left!

3 I don't usually add **much** / **many** salt when I'm cooking.

4 There's only **a little** / **a few** coffee in the jar.

5 I only have **a little** / **a few** recipe books.

5 Complete the sentences with a, an, the or Ø (zero article).

1 Do you like <u>Ø</u> strawberries?

2 I need ___ glass of water.

3 Where's ___ cake that I bought yesterday?

4 Would you like ___ orange?

5 I don't usually have ___ sugar in my coffee.

6 Would you like ___ slice of bread?

6 Circle the correct words.

As you know, I love writing about **Ø** / **the** food. I don't go to **many** / **lot** restaurants, so when a friend invited me to **a** / **an** new Spanish restaurant called El Sabor, I said yes. It was fantastic! There were **much** / **a lot** of really delicious dishes to choose from. **The** / **Ø** desserts were amazing! My only complaint was that they didn't bring us **some** / **any** bread to eat with our meal.

For more help, go to the Grammar reference:
→ **Student's Book** pages 204–206

LISTENING

→ Go to page 99 to read the audioscript.

> ✓ **HELPFUL HINT FOR THIS TASK**
>
> - Read each question and <u>underline</u> the key words.
> - Draw lines between A and B.
> - Listen carefully and use the script if necessary.

1 🔊 06 **Listen to the first part of an interview with Elsa, a food journalist, about <u>a restaurant in New York</u>. What is <u>different</u> about this restaurant?**

A   All the cooks are grandmothers.

B   You don't have to pay for the food.

2 🔊 07 **Listen to the rest of the interview and circle the correct answers.**

1   How did Elsa learn about this restaurant?
  Ⓐ   A friend told her about it.
  B   She read a review of it online.

2   Mr Scaravella started the restaurant because
  A   he was fed up with eating in expensive restaurants.
  B   he wanted to remember his own grandmother's food.

3   What do we learn about the menu?
  A   There are dishes from a different country every night.
  B   Some of the dishes are not very popular.

4   The different women who cook at the restaurant
  A   all compete with each other to make the best dishes.
  B   give each other new ideas for cooking.

5   What do we learn about the cooking classes at the restaurant?
  A   You have to book in advance.
  B   They are free.

6   What did Elsa most enjoy about the experience?
  A   the food
  B   the atmosphere

✔ **HELPFUL HINT FOR THIS TASK**

- Read the question and highlight the key words.
- Number the paragraphs.
- Read the missing sentences. Use colours to highlight key words.
- Find similar or related words in the text.

Five sentences have been removed from the text below.

For each question, choose the correct answer.

There are three extra sentences which you do not need to use.

Sweets – an ancient product

In a cave near Valencia in Spain there are paintings of people climbing trees to collect and eat the honey from bees' nests. Experts have studied these and reached the conclusion that they are eight thousand years old. (1) _C_ And that's not hard to understand because, for most people today, eating sweets is a very enjoyable thing to do.

The next time that sweet foods appear in history is around four thousand years ago in India. We know this from ancient texts that were written at that time in the Sanskrit language. (2) _____ Sadly though, no-one knows exactly what they tasted like. We also know that the ancient Egyptians, Greeks and Romans all loved sweets, which they made by rolling fruit or nuts in honey. However, we now know that sugar was available in ancient Rome. (3) _____ For this reason, sugar wasn't used for making sweets but for adding to medicines.

In Europe in the Middle Ages (6th–16th centuries) the price of sugar meant that sweets were only for very rich people. (4) _____ They could earn lots of money from having their own shop or from working in the palaces of kings and queens. Sweets were made by hand using boiled sugar or an ingredient called marzipan. It was common at the time to create sculptures of animals, castles, trees and even people. Some of the sculptures were huge and were presented to guests at formal dinners.

The kinds of sweets we recognise today started to be made in the nineteenth century. The development of factories meant that sweets could be made in very large quantities. (5) _____ The kinds of things they were able to buy were boiled sweets, chewing gum, toffee and chocolate.

A Sweet-makers were considered to be highly skilled professionals.

B Sugar comes from a plant which is known as sugarcane.

C ~~These pictures show that people in ancient times loved eating sweet things.~~

D People believed this ingredient could cure various illnesses.

E Chocolate from Central America came to Europe in the 1500s.

F They have a lovely taste and give us lots of energy.

G This affected the price, and sweets became popular with ordinary people.

H The documents describe sweets made using milk and sugar.

For more help with Reading Part 4:
→ **Student's Book Exam Focus** page 48

1 Look at the photo above.
Circle the correct words.

I can see a family. I'm (**not sure**) / **not being sure**, but I think they're in a café, because there are spoons and forks on the table **behind** / **in front of** the glasses. There's a boy **in** / **on** the left. He **holds** / **is holding** something. I don't know what it is. It looks **as** / **like** a menu, or maybe a book. I think it's summer **so** / **because** they're wearing summer clothes.

2 Match the halves of the sentences for talking about photographs. Use different colours.

1	This is a photograph	A	some cakes on the table.
2	There are	B	see four people.
3	I can	C	of a café.

4	She's holding something. It looks	D	for serving water.
5	I don't know what	E	they're called.
6	People use them	F	like a large jug.

WRITING

1 Complete the time expressions in the sentences with the correct words.

| later | After | end | ~~last~~ | When | At |

1 I went out for a meal ___last___ weekend.

2 _____ the waiter arrived, she seemed very friendly.

3 _____ first, the food tasted a bit strange.

4 _____ a while, I started to enjoy it.

5 At the _____ of the meal, I felt very happy.

6 Our food arrived half an hour _____.

2 Circle the correct time expressions in the story.

I invited some friends to my flat for a meal **after a while / last Saturday**. I like cooking, so I was happy to cook a meal for everyone. **When they arrived / Next**, we sat down at the table and I brought the food out. We started eating, but **at first / then** everyone started coughing. There was too much pepper in the food! I brought some water, but it was no good. **After a while / At the end of the meal**, we decided that we really couldn't eat it. I was a bit upset **at first / next**, but then I saw the funny side of it. **Next / At first**, we had to decide what to do! We decided to order some pizzas, and we had a great evening together.

Match the idioms with their meaning. Draw lines. Use different colours.

1	It's a piece of cake.	A	He told them all about it!
2	Take it with a pinch of salt.	B	It's really easy!
3	He spilt the beans.	C	You definitely shouldn't believe that.

4	It's all gone pear shaped.	D	I don't like that kind of thing.
5	It's no good crying over spilt milk.	E	Everything's gone wrong.
6	It's not my cup of tea.	F	It's happened and you can't change it now, so it's not worth worrying about it.

HOW WAS UNIT 3?

Gave it a go ☐

Getting there ☐

Aced it! ☐

4 CITY LIVING?

VOCABULARY

1 Complete the words in the sentences.

> apartment block   waterfall   ~~stream~~
> neighbourhood   skyscraper

1   a small **river**: s<u>tream</u>
2   the **area** where you **live**: n_____
3   a large **building** with lots of **flats** in it:
    a_____ b_____
4   **water** that falls from **high** up:
    w_____
5   a very **tall** building: s_____

2 Match the halves of the sentences. Use different colours.

1	It was easy to **get around** because	A	is to use the **subway**.
2	The quickest way to **travel** across **New York**	B	the **food truck** over there.
3	Let's buy a **burger** from	C	there were lots of **signposts** showing us where things were.

4	The city has an amazing **skyline**,	D	with **nature** all around me.
5	I love spending time **outdoors**	E	to enjoy the **beautiful scenery** around us.
6	When we got to the **top of the hill** we stopped	F	with lots of **tall buildings**.

3 Match the adjectives with what the people say about places.

> beautiful   noisy   ~~exciting~~
> peaceful   friendly   boring

1   A lot of **great** and **interesting** things happen here!   <u>exciting</u>
2   It's always **quiet** here. _____
3   The people are very **kind** here.
    _____
4   **Nothing** ever **happens** here!
    _____
5   This place **looks** really **lovely**.
    _____
6   It's **never quiet** here! _____

Need help? ➔ **Student's Book** page 54

GRAMMAR

Scan the QR code and watch the grammar animation.

> If an activity in the past **is interrupted by an event**, we often introduce the event with when.
> I was having my lunch **when** he called me.
>
> We can introduce the **background** with while.
> He called me **while** I was having my lunch.
> **While** I was having my lunch, he called me.

1 Complete the text with the correct past simple or past continuous form of the verbs.

It **(rain)** __was raining__ when I **(arrive)** ___arrived___ at Jo's apartment block, so I quickly **(run)** _____ up to the first floor and **(ring)** _____ the doorbell. While I **(wait)** _____ for Jo to open the door, I **(check)** _____ my phone. Yes, it was the right day and time for the party. I was surprised when there was no answer. While I **(think)** _____ about what to do next, I **(see)** _____ another friend arriving. 'Hi,' I said. 'Jo's not in.' 'But you're at the wrong flat,' he said. 'Jo lives on the second floor.'

2 Join the sentences using when or while.

1 The taxi arrived __while__ I **was having** a shower.

2 I was waiting for the bus __when__ I **saw** Sam.

3 Lia met Paul _____ she **was living** in London.

4 I was cooking dinner _____ Maria **called** me.

5 It started raining _____ we **were walking** home.

6 George was driving home _____ his car **broke** down.

We use the past perfect to talk about something that happened **before or after another** past event.

We make the past perfect with **had / hadn't** + the **past participle**.

We often use the past perfect with **never, ever, already** and **just**. We put the words between **had** and the **past participle**.

---

3 Complete the sentences with the correct past perfect form of the verbs.

1 The film **(start)** __had__ already __started__ when we got to the cinema.

2 Max **(leave)** _____ just _____ the house when I called.

3 I was excited because I **(try)** _____ never _____ waterskiing before.

4 I didn't go for a pizza because I **(not bring)** _____ _____ enough money with me.

5 **(visit)** _____ you ever _____ the United States before you went to study there?

4 Complete the text with the correct past simple or past perfect form of the verbs.

I **(go)** __went__ to Rome last summer. I **(visit)** __had__ never __visited__ Italy before, so I was really excited, and I wasn't disappointed! The ancient buildings **(look)** _____ amazing! I **(find)** _____ it hard to believe that people **(build)** _____ _____ them so long ago, without any modern machines! We **(have)** _____ some great pizzas, and I was really pleased because I **(learn)** _____ _____ a few phrases in Italian before I went, and I **(manage)** _____ to use them while I was there.

For more help, go to the Grammar reference:
→ **Student's Book** pages 206–208

Circle the correct verb forms.

Last summer, my aunt and uncle **took** / **were taking** me for a walk in the countryside while I **was staying** / **had stayed** with them. It was terrible! First, my feet **got** / **had got** wet because I **wasn't bringing** / **hadn't brought** any strong shoes with me. Then some cows **ran** / **were running** after us while we **were walking** / **had walked** through a field. Finally, **we spent** / **had spent** hours trying to find our way back because my uncle **was forgetting** / **had forgotten** to bring the map with him. I think I'll stay in the city this year!

READING

✓ HELPFUL HINT FOR THIS TASK

- Read the questions and highlight the key words.
- Number the paragraphs.
- Find similar or related words in the text.

1 Read the article about green skyscrapers. What does the article discuss? Choose A or B.

A   the reasons why green skyscrapers are still not very popular

B   the advantages and disadvantages of green skyscrapers

1 The country in the city?

Cities are often noisy and dirty places, and many people prefer the peaceful atmosphere of the countryside, with open fields, and forests. However, **there are many good reasons to live in cities – jobs, exciting things to do and plenty of new people to meet**. Some architects are now trying to bring the country into the city, by creating 'green skyscrapers'.

The Bosco Verticale in Milan is a skyscraper which tries to create a 'forest in the sky'. It opened in 2014 and has two towers, one just over 100 metres high and the other around 80 metres high. Inside, it is mainly apartments, but there are also some offices. The special thing about this skyscraper is that there are nearly **1,000 trees, and also hundreds of smaller plants**, growing all over it.

Skyscrapers like this are more difficult and more expensive to build. There are problems with planting trees so high up – **not all kinds of trees can live in the strong winds at this height**. Also, someone has to look after the plants, to water them in hot weather and cut them back when they grow too big, so they don't spoil the view for the people who live there. This could be a lot of work for the people who live there, but at Bosco Verticale, **a special team of professional gardeners takes care of it.**

But green skyscrapers also bring a lot of benefits. The trees and plants clean the air, keep the apartments cool in hot weather and reduce the amount of noise that people hear inside the building. **More importantly, most people would agree that they are much more attractive to look at** than the usual metal and glass. Some architects believe that over the next 20 years green buildings could change the skyline of our cities, to make them look more like forests.

I visited Singapore recently, and stayed in the Parkroyal on Pickering hotel. This 'hotel in a garden' is a great example of a green skyscraper. The building is covered in plants, and there is a 'skygarden', where guests can sit and enjoy views of the city. There are plants everywhere, and **I was amazed that there are even indoor waterfalls!** Rooms aren't cheap, but the price is worth paying to get the chance to escape from the noise and dirt outside and enjoy a little bit of the countryside in the heart of the city.

2 Read the article again. (Circle) the correct answers.

1 In the first paragraph, what **does the writer say about cities**?
  (A) There are a lot of benefits to living in cities.
  B There are too many new buildings in cities.

2 What do we learn about **Bosco Verticale**?
  A There are only apartments inside.
  B It has trees and other plants growing on it.

3 Why are **some trees not suitable** to use in green skyscrapers?
  A They don't like the weather conditions.
  B They are too expensive.

4 What do we **learn about the plants** at Bosco Verticale?
  A They often cause problems when they get too big.
  B People are paid to look after them.

5 According to the writer, what is the **biggest advantage** of green skyscrapers?
  A They keep the apartments cool.
  B They look nicer than other buildings.

6 How did the **writer feel** about staying in the Parkroyal on Pickering hotel?
  A disappointed at the views from the skygarden
  B surprised that there are waterfalls inside the hotel

LISTENING PART 1

→ 🎧 Go to page 100 to read the audioscript.

> ✅ **HELPFUL HINT FOR THIS TASK**
>
> - Read the questions and <u>underline</u> the key words.
> - Look at the pictures and write the words if you know them.
> - Use a blank piece of paper to cover the pictures in the other questions as you listen.
> - Remember you listen twice.

🎧 08 **For each question, (circle) the correct answer.**

1   <u>Where</u> will the woman go <u>camping this summer</u>?

A   **(B)**   C

2   What is the view from the apartment block?

A   B   C

3   Which activity did the woman help with?

A   B   C

4   Where will the friends meet before going to the theatre?

A   B   C

5   Where is the problem in the apartment building?

A   B   C

6   What did the woman do in the park?

A   B   C

7   Where in the city will they eat tonight?

A   B   C

For more help with Listening Part 1:
→ **Student's Book Exam Focus** page 60

SPEAKING

1 Complete the words in the conversations.

> ~~about~~ sounds sure Shall idea
> that's could

1 A: What do you want to do today?
  B: What a<u>bout</u> going to the park? There's a concert there this afternoon.
  A: That s_____ good.

2 A: S_____ we go to the beach this afternoon?
  B: I'm not s_____ . It isn't very warm!

3 A: It's a lovely evening. We c_____ have a barbecue!
  B: That's a nice i_____ . I'll invite some friends.
  A: Yes, t_____ great!

2 (Circle) the correct answers.

1 We could go for a pizza if you like.
  A Yes, I like.
  (B) That sounds good.

2 What about watching a movie tonight?
  A That was great.
  B I think that's a good idea.

3 Shall we organise a party?
  A I'm not sure.
  B That's good.

4 Let's meet at 7.30.
  A That looks good.
  B Yes, that's great.

5 We could go ice skating.
  A I don't think that's a better idea.
  B Hmm, I don't really like that idea.

WRITING

1 Complete the words.

> later end first ~~next~~ after

1 We walked round the shops all afternoon, and the **n**<u>ext</u> day, my feet really hurt!

2 We visited the art gallery and **a**_____ that we went for a coffee.

3 I was really worried, but in the **e**_____ everything was fine.

4 At **f**_____ I thought Freddie was joking, but then I realised he was serious.

5 I saw Sara again **l**_____, at the sports centre.

2 (Circle) the correct time linkers.

It was my birthday on Saturday. **(While)** / **At first** I was getting dressed in the morning, the doorbell rang. I opened the door, and **in the end** / **then** I saw a big group of my friends. 'We're taking you out,' they said. We went for a coffee first, and **next** / **at first** we went to a big theme park near the town. **When** / **After that** we went back into town for something to eat. **Later** / **When**, we all went back to one friend's flat and we watched a movie together. I was really tired but happy when I **in the end** / **finally** got home. It was an amazing day.

HOW WAS UNIT 4?

Gave it a go   ☐

Getting there   ☐

Aced it!   ☐

5 PICTURE OF HEALTH

VOCABULARY

1 **Read the clues below. Look at the image. Write the words.**

> ~~skin~~ arm knee shoulder lung
> ankle

1 It's all over your body.

2 It's at the top of your arm.

3 You use it when you breathe.

4 You move it when you wave your hand.

5 You bend it if you want to jump.

6 It joins your foot to your leg.

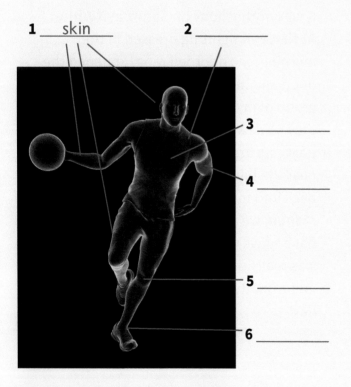

1 ___skin___   2 _____

3 _____

4 _____

5 _____

6 _____

Need help? → **Student's Book** page 64

2 **Complete what Marco says about his health with the correct words.**

> ~~ill~~ sore throat earache cold
> backache cough

I feel really __ill__ today. I think I've got a bad _____ . I've got a terrible _____ _____, so I **can't eat** or drink anything, and I've also got a _____, which gets worse every time I speak. I've got _____ in both my **ears**, and I can't walk around very much because I've got _____ ! The only thing I can really do comfortably is lie on my bed and play computer games!

3 **Circle the correct words.**

1 Be careful, or you'll **injure** / **pain** yourself.

2 What happened to your arm? Is it **pains** / **painful**?

3 Don't lift that heavy box – you might **sore** / **hurt** your back.

4 My arm is really **injury** / **sore** from falling off my bike.

5 I think you should go to the hospital – that looks like a serious **hurt** / **injury**.

6 If you've still got a **pain** / **hurt** in your head tomorrow, maybe you should go to the doctor.

4 **Complete the words in the notice.**

prescription   emergency   ~~patients~~
tablets   infection

Important notice

If you have an appointment with the doctor, please wait in the waiting area. There may be other p<u>atients</u> before you, so please wait until your name is called.

If the doctor gives you a **p**_____, you can collect your medicines at the chemist's on Broad Street. Parents please note, the doctors usually recommend liquid medicines for children. If you would prefer **t**_____ for your child, please tell the doctor.

If you are seriously ill and think the situation is an **e**_____, please speak to the receptionist and she will call an ambulance.

If you have an **i**_____ which might be dangerous to other people, please do NOT come to the clinic. Call us, and we will arrange for the doctor to visit you at home.

Need help? → **Student's Book** page 67

GRAMMAR

Scan the QR code and watch the grammar animation.

1 **Match the sentences that have the same meaning. Use different colours.**

1	I wasn't able to ride a bike when I was younger.	A	Most animals can swim quite well.
2	Most animals are able to swim quite well.	B	I could ski when I was six years old!
3	I was able to ski when I was six years old!	C	I couldn't ride a bike when I was younger.

4	My baby cousin is able to walk now.	D	My grandma can't run marathons anymore.
5	I wasn't able to finish the race.	E	My baby cousin can walk now.
6	My grandma isn't able to run marathons anymore.	F	I couldn't finish the race.

2 **Circle the correct words.**

1 You should **do** / **to do** more exercise.

2 I think you **ought to** / **ought** go to bed earlier.

3 You shouldn't **eating** / **eat** so much chocolate.

4 I don't think you **ought to** / **don't ought to** spend so much time playing on your computer.

5 You **should** / **ought** take plenty of breaks when you're studying.

6 You **shouldn't** / **don't ought to** drink so many sweet drinks.

3 ⊘Circle the correct words to complete the posts.

Abi44G   I want to get fit quickly. I'm really unfit at the moment, and I **can't** / **couldn't** even run for a bus! I **'m not able to** / **shouldn't** get to a gym because there isn't one near my house. Any ideas?

MaxPP   You **ought** / **should** start slowly and build up your fitness over a few months. Try walking to start with, and soon you **were able to** / **'ll be able to** run!

SamT99   You **shouldn't** / **could** worry about not being near a gym. There's lots of gym equipment that you **can** / **shouldn't** use at home, and it isn't expensive if you buy second-hand. Stop making excuses!

FitAmy   You definitely **ought to** / **can't** get a bike. I **weren't able to** / **couldn't** even ride a bike six months ago, but now I cycle everywhere, and it's a really great way to get fit!

Scan the QR code and watch the grammar animation.

4 ⊘Circle the correct words.

My top tips for marathon training

The first thing to do is stop delaying and start training! If you **couldn't** / **aren't able to** run very far when you start, don't worry — everyone **could** / **has to** start somewhere. You **must** / **need** have a training programme — that's really important. The main idea of your programme is to slowly increase the distance you **could** / **can** comfortably run, until a marathon doesn't seem such a scary idea. You **should** / **are able to** try to run at least three times a week. In the last two weeks before the marathon, you **need** / **ought to** do less, not more. This sounds crazy, but you really mustn't get an injury just before the big race.

5 Complete the gym rules. Use must / mustn't, have to or need to.

GYM RULES

1   All members __must__ have their membership cards with them at all times.

2   You don't __need to__ book classes in advance, but it is a good idea for popular classes.

3   Junior members under 14 _____ use the pool without an adult.

4   All members _____ ask for permission from a member of staff before using the heaviest weights.

5   Please use a gym towel when exercising. You don't _____ bring your own – you can get one at the reception desk.

6   Remember, our staff _____ know if you have a health problem. Please don't forget to tell us!

For more help, go to the Grammar reference:
→ **Student's Book** pages 208–210

READING PART 6

> ✅ **HELPFUL HINT FOR THIS TASK**
>
> - Highlight the words before and after the gap.
> - Think about what words they could be.
> - Read through the text and then complete the gaps.

For each question, write the correct answer.

Write one word for each gap.

To: Laura
Subject: Poor you!
Reply Forward

Hi,

I'm really sorry to hear you broke your leg during the half-marathon on Saturday. You poor thing!

I was so surprised to get your email because you've **(1)** _never_ had an accident while running before. As you say, at least **(2)** _____ were lots of people around you to help. And it was lucky you didn't have to wait **(3)** _____ long time for the ambulance to arrive to take you to the hospital. Did the doctor say how long **(4)** _____ will be before you can run again?

Would you like me to **(5)** _____ some shopping for you, cook you a meal or take you to your hospital appointments? Just let me know if I can help **(6)** _____ all.

Janie

For more help with Reading Part 6:
→ **Student's Book Exam Focus** page 73

LISTENING

→ 🔊 Go to page 101 to read the audioscript.

1 🔊 09 **Which app does Jake suggest for Elly?**

A Daily Fit Club

B Superfit in Ten

> ✅ **HELPFUL HINT FOR THIS TASK**
>
> - <u>Underline</u> the key words in each sentence.
> - Think about what words the speaker might use instead of these words.

2 🔊 09 **Listen again. Write ✓ (true) or ✗ (false).**

1 Elly thinks she is <u>already</u> quite <u>fit</u>.

   not as fit as I should be _____ **✗**

2 With <u>Ten Minute Yoga</u>, you do the <u>same exercises</u> each <u>day</u>. _____

3 **Daily Fit Club** is good for people who **haven't done much exercise** before. _____

4 Jake says that the workouts on **Burn the Fat** seem **very quick**. _____

5 Jake thinks most people would find **Burn the Fat boring**. _____

6 The **first** workouts on **Superfit in Ten** are the **most difficult**. _____

7 Jake says Elly will only **get fitter** if she exercises **regularly**. _____

SPEAKING

1 Read and write:

A	for asking about problems.
S	for showing sympathy.
G	for giving advice.

1 What's wrong? A

2 Get well soon. ___

3 You ought to stay in bed today. ___

4 Take care. ___

5 Why don't you go and see the doctor? ___

6 How about having a nice hot drink? ___

7 It's a good idea to put ice on an injury like that. ___

2 Complete the conversations with the correct words.

~~how~~   ~~better~~

A: Hi, Amy, __how__ are you?

B: Not very well. I think I've got flu.

A: Oh, I hope you feel _better_ soon.

you   matter   sorry

A: Hi, George. You look terrible! What's the _____?

B: I've got a really bad headache.

A: I'm _____ to hear that. If I were _____, I'd go home and go to bed.

after   Poor

A: Oh, my leg's still really sore from the injury I got on Saturday.

B: _____ you! Why don't you go home and rest it?

A: I can't today. I have to go to work. But I'll rest tomorrow.

B: Well, look _____ yourself!

A: Thanks, I will.

Match the sentence halves.

1	I've got a **splitting**	A	**on** my feet.
2	Lots of people are ill at the moment. I think there's **a**	B	**headache**.
3	I was in bed all last week, but now I'm **back**	C	**bug** going around.

4	I don't feel well. I think I'm **coming**	D	**feet** are killing me.
5	Jill's been really ill, but luckily she's on **the**	E	**mend** now.
6	I've walked 30 kilometres today, and now **my**	F	**down** with flu.

2 Complete the email with the correct words.

> don't for it's You're don't
> I'm ~~for~~ after

Hi Jan

Thanks __for__ your email. You _____ need to worry about me now – _____ feeling much better. _____ definitely right that I should still rest, though. I _____ want to, but I know it's good _____ me.

Dan's been brilliant. He's really looked _____ me well! I've got some new medicine now – I can't remember its name, but _____ really good, so I hope I might be better soon.

Emma

WRITING

1 Circle the correct words.

1 I hurt a **muscle** / **wrist** in my leg.

2 Your elbow is in the **shoulder** / **middle** of your arm.

3 You need your **ankle** / **tongue** to speak.

4 I try to eat **healthy** / **sick** food.

5 My lungs hurt when I **breathe** / **cough** in.

HOW WAS UNIT 5?

Gave it a go ☐

Getting there ☐

Aced it! ☐

6 ONLINE, OFFLINE

VOCABULARY

1 Complete the words in the sentences.

> request ~~post~~ selfie block
> comment ~~follow~~ tag

1 When you **p**ost___ a **photo** or **piece of writing**, you put it **online**.

2 If you **f**ollow___ **someone**, you see all the **updates** that they put on **Instagram**.

3 If you send someone a **friend r_____** , you **ask** them to be a **friend online**.

4 When you **t_____ someone**, you **add** their **name** to a **photo**.

5 If you **b_____ someone**, you **stop** them **seeing photos** and **things** you write.

6 A **s_____** is a **photo** you take of **yourself**.

7 A **c_____** is **something** you **write** when a **friend** has put something **online**.

2 Circle the correct words.

1 Carl was being really annoying online, so I **updated** / **unfriended** him.

2 Hana's just posted a new **story** / **filter** about her trip to Paris.

3 I don't change my online **status** / **hashtag** very often.

4 How often do you **update** / **request** your social media?

Need help? → **Student's Book** page 81

3 Complete the posts with the correct phrasal verbs.

> ~~broke up~~ grew apart rely on
> turn to get on make up

LolaB I'm feeling a bit sad because I _broke___ __up___ with my boyfriend last month. We gradually _____ _____ and I decided to end the relationship. I don't want to _____ _____ with him again, but I miss him and I can't imagine meeting anyone else. Any ideas?

TomG77 Why don't you _____ _____ your friends for help? See if they can introduce you to someone new, and you never know – you might hit it off!

MiaKat I don't agree with TomG. It isn't fair to _____ _____ friends to find you a new boyfriend. Why not try a dating app? There's definitely someone out there that you can _____ _____ well with! Good luck!

Need help? → **Student's Book** page 85

GRAMMAR

Scan the QR codes and watch the grammar animations. a b

1 Complete the conversations with the correct form of will or going to.

1 A: When __are__ __you__ __going__ __to__ **move** to London?

B: I'm not sure. I need to find a flat first.

A: Oh, I _____ **help** you look!

2 A: _____ Harry _____ _____ **come** for a meal with us tomorrow?

B: I don't know. Maybe I _____ **text** him later to invite him.

3 A: What's that?

B: It's a book about apps. I _____ _____ _____ **do** a course next year on how to develop new apps.

A: That sounds interesting.

B: I _____ **lend** you the book if you like.

2 Circle the correct verb forms.

1 Don't forget we **go** / **'re going** to the cinema this evening. The film **starts** / **'s starting** at seven, so don't be late!

2 What **do you do** / **are you doing** tomorrow evening?

3 Where are you? You should be here at the station with me. The train **leaves** / **'s leaving** in 10 minutes!

4 Sorry, I can't come to football training with you this evening. I **meet** / **'m meeting** Emma.

5 Can't chat now. I need to get some food and the supermarket **closes** / **'s closing** at six.

6 **Do you see** / **Are you seeing** Paul tomorrow? If so, can you remind him he owes me some money?

3 Circle the correct form of will or going to.

1 Oh, no! It's 8.30 already. I **'m going to** / 'll miss my train!

2 I think travel will / **is going to** be more expensive in the future. People won't travel much.

3 Look at the sky! I think it will / **is going to rain**.

4 Sam works really hard, so it's obvious that he will / **is going to** pass all his exams.

4 Circle the correct verbs.

So, college **starts** / will start again today. This year is my final year, so I know it **is** / **is going to be** difficult. I want to do well, so I **'ll work** / **'m going to** work really hard, especially at English. I **'ll meet** / **'m meeting** my English teacher this afternoon to talk about things I can do at home to help me improve. I'm sure she **'ll have** / **'s having** some good ideas. As part of my plan, I **'ll stop** / **'m going to stop** using social media so much.

For more help, go to the Grammar reference:

→ **Student's Book** pages 210–211

→ Go to page 102 to read the audioscript.

> ✓ **HELPFUL HINT FOR THIS TASK**
>
> • Read the question carefully.
> • Highlight the key words.
> • Try and predict what the answers will be by looking at the words before and after the spaces.
> • Don't write more than two words.
> • You can write dates and times as numbers.

🔊 **10 You will hear a journalist called Steffi talking about a week she spent without using social media.**

For each question, write the correct answer in the gap.

Write one or two words or a date or a time.

Steffi's Week without Social Media

Steffi started using social media at
(1) ___university___ .

Steffi mainly used social media for posting
(2) _____ .

Steffi realised she was spending at least
(3) _____ every day on social media.

When she gave up social media, Steffi read a
(4) _____ instead.

After one week without social media, Steffi felt less **(5)** _____ .

Steffi now plans to use a **(6)** _____ app once a day.

For more help with Listening Part 3:
→ **Student's Book Exam Focus** page 73

> ✓ **HELPFUL HINT FOR THIS TASK**
>
> • Look at the highlighted words in the questions.
> • Read the questions and <u>underline</u> the key words.
> • <u>Underline</u> the key words in each paragraph that relate to the key words in the questions.

1 **Read the article about the future of social media.**

Choose the best heading for each section A–D.

1 Bringing the world **closer together**

2 ~~The end of the~~ **~~screen~~**

3 New ways to **hang out** with friends

4 **Connected** to everything and everyone

What's the future of social media? Read the opinions of four experts.

Twenty-five years ago there was no social media – no Facebook or Instagram, no tweets or sharing of photos. Social media has changed our lives a lot, but where will it be in twenty years' time? We asked four experts.

A 2

Technology will all use voice controls, so there won't be any more keyboards on our phones. **Screens won't be important either**, so wanting the latest smartphones with bigger and better screens will be a **thing of the past**. Instead, we will see holograms – images in the real world, in front of us, and they will look amazingly real. At the moment we chat with a friend, and we look at their face on our phone or computer. In 20 years, we'll be able to see them sitting next to us, looking very much like a real person.

Jacob Stone, Media Director

B __

I think we will definitely have an electronic device inside our body which will connect us to everything around us. We will be **connected to the machines** in our homes and places of work, like our printers and cookers. We'll be connected to the internet too, so we'll be able to find information just by thinking about it. And, of course, **we'll be connected to each other**. I know it sounds a bit crazy at the moment, but I really believe it will be possible to share our thoughts and feelings with each other directly, even when we're in different parts of the world.

Alyssa Tyrone, Creative Manager

C __

When events happen anywhere in the world, we won't need to send journalists to report on them. There will be hundreds of films, stories and messages from **normal people** who are there, **showing the world** what's happening, as it actually happens. People will also **be able to share smells** and tastes, and even feelings, so it will be possible for everyone to **really experience what is happening in another part of the world**, whether it's a terrible flood or a fire, a big sporting event or a cultural celebration. We will all feel more connected to each other, and the world will feel a much smaller place.

Amelia Smid, Digital News Editor

D __

At the moment, I connect with my friends on social media by liking posts, writing comments and uploading photos. In 20 years, I'll disconnect from all this. I'll put on my special glasses and **meet my friends in virtual worlds**. It will be possible to choose the place, from a beach in Spain to a café in London, and I'll bring together people from my real life and my online friends to have social time together. We'll chat and share jokes, and the experience will feel completely real, even though we'll really all be in different places.

Sajid Khan, Digital Product Developer

2 Read the predictions again. Which expert (A–D) thinks ...

1   we <u>won't need</u> a computer or phone to <u>search</u> for something <u>online</u>. <u>B</u>

2   we <u>won't care</u> so much about the <u>kind of phone</u> we have. __

3   we will be able to share experiences from all our senses. __

4   ordinary people will report the news for us. __

5   we will decide where in the world to see our friends. __

6   our real friends and social media friends will meet each other. __

PUSH YOURSELF B2

Complete the sentences.

probably	~~chance~~ chance certainly definitely

1 There's a <u>chance</u> computers will become even smaller.

2 People will _____ travel to Mars one day.

3 We _____ won't stop using our phones.

4 There's a _____ cities will become smaller.

5 People will _____ eat less meat in the future.

SPEAKING

1 (Circle) the correct answers.

1 Where do you live?
   A I live in Berlin.
   B I'd like to visit Paris one day.

2 What do you do?
   A A lot of people work for a bank.
   B I work for a bank.

3 How do you get to school every day?
   A I sometimes walk if the weather's fine.
   B 300 people work in my office.

4 Do you think English will be useful for you in the future? Why? / Why not?
   A You need English for a lot of different jobs.
   B I'd like to learn some other languages in the future.

5 What does your family do together?
   A We sometimes go out for meals.
   B Some of my friends don't get on well with their families.

2 Highlight the phrases for gaining time.

1 A: What do you like doing in your free time?
   B: Oh, lots of things. Let me see, I really enjoy doing sport, and …

2 A: Tell us about the place where you live.
   B: Hmm, the place where I live. It's a small town in the north of Italy …

3 A: How much time do you spend on social media?
   B: Well, to be honest, I don't spend very much time on social media. I …

4 A: What do you like about your job or school?
   B: Hmm, what I like about my job. I guess I meet a lot of people and I really enjoy that because …

5 A: Where do you meet your friends?
   B: OK, so, I have a lot of friends and we often meet …

6 A: What do you find difficult about learning English?
   B: Hmm, what I find difficult. I think probably the most difficult thing for me is …

WRITING

1 Circle the correct words to complete the tips for writing a blog post.

1 It's a **good** / **bad** idea to show your own personality in what you write.

2 You should **use your own style** / **copy a successful style**.

3 Try to write **long** / **short** paragraphs so it doesn't get boring.

4 Use **a formal** / **an informal** tone.

5 **Ask questions** / **Make general statements** to help the reader feel involved.

6 **Invite** / **Don't invite** comments from your readers.

2 Read the sentences from a blog post about friends.

Use different colours to match the halves of the sentences.

1	Everyone understands the importance of **friends** in our lives.	A	Sometimes you just know that someone will be a friend **for life**.
2	There are times when you rely on a friend **to give you support**.	B	It's hard to imagine life without **friends**, isn't it?
3	Sometimes you can recognise immediately that you will have a **long friendship** with someone.	C	When **things go wrong**, you can see who your real friends are.

4	Friends share both **good** and **bad** experiences with you.	D	Friends are there for you in **good** times and **bad**.
5	Some of your friends may **find it difficult** to have good relationships with each other.	E	Sometimes you really need a friend **to help you**.
6	When you are experiencing **problems**, it is clear which of your friends are true friends.	F	Some of your friends may **not hit it off** with each other.

3 Tick (✓) the two openings that would make you keep reading.

A Let me start by telling you one of my funniest social media stories.

B This post will discuss the history of social media and its importance in the world today.

C Do you love the way you can connect with people on social media? I certainly do! So, what new forms of social media are coming soon, and how will we use them?

HOW WAS UNIT 6?

Gave it a go	☐
Getting there	☐
Aced it!	☐

7 WHAT'S YOUR STYLE?

VOCABULARY

1 Complete the words in the conversation.

suit	fit	look	~~style~~	afford	try

A: Oh, look at that dress! I love that long s<u>tyle</u> and the colour would really s_____ you. You l_____ great in blue! Why don't you t_____ it on?

B: It's lovely, but the only size they've got is small, and I don't think that will f_____ me. Anyway, I can't a_____ to buy any more clothes!

2 Complete the online adverts with the correct words.

~~loose~~	buttons	stripes

A <u>loose</u> white shirt with blue _____ and a white collar. There are a few _____ missing, but otherwise it's in perfect condition. £3.99   **Buy it now!**

sleeves	pattern	plain

Two dresses, both with long _____, one _____ red, the other blue with a flowery _____. Only worn once, but now too tight for me. £10 each   **Buy it now!**

Need help? ➔ **Student's Book** page 90

3 Match the definitions with the words. Use different colours.

1	**not neat** or tidy	A	display
2	an **arrangement of things** for sale in a shop	B	bargain
3	**things** that are sold in a shop	C	untidy
4	another word for a **shop**	D	goods
5	something that is **reduced in price** and **seems cheaper** than it should be	E	store

4 Choose the correct words.

messy	products	~~shoppers~~	value

Most _shoppers_ will love this shop! Some of the displays in the shop window look a bit _____, but don't let that put you off. The _____ that they sell are all great, and really good _____ for money.

5 Circle the correct words.

Thank you for your recent (order) / refund from our website for a / some Superfit jeans and three other items. Your return / receipt is attached to this email. Your goods will be ordered / delivered to your home address within three days. If the goods are damaged / exchanged in any way, please exchange / return them to us and we will arrange for a full receipt / refund to be paid into your account.

Need help? ➔ **Student's Book** page 92

 **GRAMMAR**

Scan the QR code and watch
the grammar animation.

Reported speech	
present simple to past simple	go ➔ went
present continuous to past continuous	is going ➔ was going
present perfect to past perfect	has gone ➔ had gone
past simple to past perfect	went ➔ had gone
past perfect to past perfect	had gone ➔ had gone
can to **could** **will** to **would** **must** to **must** (no change)	

1 (Circle) **the correct verb forms to complete the reported speech.**

1 'I bought my dress online.'
She said that she **bought** / (**had bought**) her dress online.

2 'I never wear jeans to work!'
He said that he never **wore** / **has worn** jeans to work.

3 'I can't afford to buy a lot of clothes.'
She said that she **can't afford** / **couldn't afford** to buy a lot of clothes.

4 'I've seen some great bargains in the sales.'
He said that he **had seen** / **saw** some great bargains in the sales.

5 'I'm trying to find some comfortable shoes.'
He said that he **was trying** / **had tried** to find some comfortable shoes.

6 'I hadn't been to that shopping centre before.'
He said that he **didn't go** / **hadn't been** to that shopping centre before.

2 **Match direct speech with reported speech. Use different colours.**

Direct speech		Reported speech	
1	We**'ve spent** all our money!	A	I said to Dan that I **could** help him choose some new trainers.
2	I**'d never been** to that shop before.	B	My friends said that they **had spent** all their money.
3	I **can** help you choose some new trainers.	C	Anna said that **she had never been** to that shop before.

4	I**'ll lend** you my jacket.	D	Mia told me that **she loved** my new shirt.
5	I **love** your new shirt.	E	Paul said that he **must** get some new trainers.
6	I **must** get some new trainers!	F	I told Maria that I **would lend** her my jacket.

3 (Circle) **the correct reported speech.**

1	Direct speech	Reported speech
	Paul: Where are you going?	Paul asked me where **I'm going** / (**I was going.**)

2	Anna: Do you like my new dress?	Anna asked me if I **like** / **liked** her new dress.

3	Eva: What have you bought?	Eva asked me what I **bought** / **had bought**.

4 (Circle) **say, said** or **tell, told.**

1 Eve **said** / (**told**) me that she wasn't interested in fashion.

2 Carl **said** / **told** that the department store had some great bargains.

3 She didn't want to **say** / **tell** me how much she had paid for her boots.

4 The shop assistant **said** / **told** to me that the bag was very popular.

For more help, go to the Grammar reference:
→ **Student's Book** pages 211–214

LISTENING

→ 🔊 Go to page 103 to read the audioscript.

✅ **HELPFUL HINT FOR THIS TASK**

- Read the questions / sentences before listening.
- <u>Underline</u> the key words.
- Think about the words you might hear.
- Listen and answer.

---

1 🔊 11 **Listen to the first part of a podcast about clothes.**

What are ethical clothes?

A expensive clothes that are very fashionable and look good on people

B clothes that are made in a way that doesn't harm the environment or people

2 🔊 12 **Listen to the rest of the podcast.**

Choose the sentence that sums up the ideas.

A Ethical clothes are good for the planet and people, and they also look good.

B Ethical clothes sound like a good idea, but they don't really exist.

3 🔊 12 **Listen again. Write ✓ (true) or ✗ (false).**

1 The trainers are made with plastic waste from the oceans. ✓

2 The company no longer uses paper bags in its stores. ____

3 Most clothes stay in the ground for hundreds of years. ____

4 The Swedish company's clothes break down in the ground. ____

5 People can't rent the Swedish company's clothes. ____

6 GoodClothes.com are suitable for vegetarians because they don't contain any animal products. ____

7 A T-shirt from GoodClothes.com is cheap. ____

READING PART 1

✔ HELPFUL HINT FOR THIS TASK

- Look at the highlighted words in the questions and the paragraphs.
- Draw lines between A, B and C.
- Underline the key words in each paragraph that relate to the options in the questions.

For each question, circle the correct answer.

1

These headphones can only be returned for a refund if the plastic box is unopened and in perfect condition.

A You won't be able to get your money back if you've damaged the box.

B If you don't like these headphones after using them, return them for a refund.

C These headphones are in the sale because the plastic box they're in is damaged.

2

Wash at 30 degrees by hand or in machine, using any cleaning liquid suitable for silk. Always wash separately and dry flat.

A After washing this shirt by hand, hang it up to dry.

B Avoid washing this shirt together with other clothes.

C Always use the recommended cleaning product when washing this shirt.

3

Welcome to Unique Fashions – the newest store on the web! Click here for a free gift in exchange for signing up to our weekly email.

A Unique Fashions are offering rewards to everyone placing their first web order.

B Customers who order online from Unique Fashions this week will receive a reward.

C There is a reward for anyone who agrees to receive emails from Unique Fashions.

4

Daisy, I went to the 50% off sale at Greens Department Store. The jeans you bought were all gone but I got some fantastic bargains in the sports department, including a pair of trainers. Morgan

A Morgan found fewer bargains in the department store sale than Daisy did.

B Morgan bought something different to her friend Daisy in the sale.

C Morgan managed to buy some trainers at less than half the original price.

5

Need a different size?
Our changing room staff will be pleased to fetch this for you. Just ask.

A If you find something is too tight, changing room staff can bring a looser size.

B Our changing room staff are happy to check for you what size you are.

C Please give anything that's the wrong size to changing room staff when you leave.

For more help with Reading Part 1:
→ **Student's Book Exam Focus** page 72

Read the conversation between Milly and a shop assistant. (Circle) what Milly says about the conversation.

The conversation	Milly said
Milly: OK. I'll take this bag, please.	
Assistant: Lovely. Can you come to the till, please?	The shop assistant (asked) / warned me to come to the till.
Milly: Of course. Is it possible to clean the bag if it gets dirty?	
Assistant: Yes. If you need to clean it, you should use a special cleaner. We've got some here, for £6.00.	She promised / advised me to use a special cleaner on the bag.
Milly: Right. I'll take that, too.	
Assistant: Now, it's important that you don't get this bag wet, otherwise the colour might come out.	She asked / warned me not to get the bag wet.
Milly: OK. It's a present for a friend, Sara. Is it possible for her to exchange it, if she doesn't like it?	
Assistant: Of course. Keep the receipt, and if she brings it back with the receipt, we'll definitely exchange it for her.	She invited / promised to exchange the bag if Sara doesn't like it.
Milly: Thanks.	

SPEAKING

1 (Circle) the correct words to complete the responses.

1 A: I'd love to go shopping in New York.

   B: So (would) / do I.

2 A: I often get new clothes for my birthday.

   B: Also / Same here.

3 A: I don't often buy things from department stores.

   B: Me also / neither.

4 A: I think it's much easier to shop online.

   B: I know what you say / mean.

5 A: I love it when the shops are really busy in the sales.

   B: Would / Do you? I hate it!

2 Choose the correct answer.

1 I don't like those trainers.

   A So do I.

   (B) Neither do I.

2 I love bright colours!

   A That's a good point.

   B Same here.

3 Sometimes it's difficult to find something that fits you.

   A Me too.

   B I know what you mean.

4 I always get excited when the sales start.

   A So do I.

   B Me neither.

WRITING

1 Match the halves of the phrases for a review. Use different colours.

1	There's a very good selection	A	is the delivery time.
2	The best thing about	B	checking out this site.
3	The only thing that's not good	C	of products.
4	It's definitely worth	D	this website is the prices.

5	I'd certainly	E	most about this site is how easy it is to use.
6	What I like	F	complaint is that you can't see pictures of all the colours.
7	My only	G	recommend this site.

2 Decide if the sentences are positive or negative. Write P or N.

1 Their products are amazing quality. __P__

2 The range is extremely limited. ___

3 Some of their things are not the best value. ___

4 There's an incredible variety of goods. ___

5 The prices are very reasonable. ___

3 Circle the correct linking words.

1 **Although** / **But** the quality is good, the range is fairly limited.

2 The staff are extremely helpful **and** / **though** they certainly know all about the products.

3 There's a great variety of products. The prices are extremely high, **as well** / **though**.

4 The staff are really friendly, **but** / **and** they're often too busy to help you.

4 Complete the review with the correct words.

recommend   but   ~~great selection~~
like most   ~~reasonable~~   complaint
worth

This is an amazing online shoe shop! There's a _great_ _selection_ of shoes and boots, and the prices are very _reasonable_. What I _____ _____ about this website is the fact that they give extra information like, 'these shoes are best for people with narrow feet.' My only _____ is that the shoes took a week to arrive, _____ I'm really pleased with them. It's definitely _____ checking out this site, and I would certainly _____ their shoes!

HOW WAS UNIT 7?

Gave it a go   ☐

Getting there   ☐

Aced it!   ☐

8 INTO THE WILD

VOCABULARY

1 Complete the words.

cave	waves	cliff	leaves	shore

1 It might be fun to explore inside here, but it's very dark. c<u>ave</u>

2 I love walking along this, next to the sea. s_____

3 If there's a storm at sea, these are very big. w_____

4 I like climbing up this and then looking down at the sea below. c_____

5 All trees have these, and they're usually green. l_____

2 Complete the sentences with the correct words.

~~branches~~ iceberg waterfall
glacier bushes sand dunes

1 There were colourful birds on the <u>branches</u> of the trees.

2 It was fun walking across the _____ _____ in the desert.

3 You can't sail your boat over the _____ !

4 There are no trees here, but there are lots of small _____ .

5 If you climb a high mountain, you may have to climb over a _____ .

6 The ship sank when it hit an _____ .

3 Read about the places. Circle the correct adjective for each place.

1 There are no sounds here at all! humid / (quiet)

2 There are so many bushes, we can't get through! dense / dry

3 There's nothing in this cave! noisy / empty

4 There's very little rain here. dry / dense

5 There are so many birds here, and they're all singing! quiet / noisy

6 It's hot here, and the air feels wet. empty / humid

Need help? → Student's Book page 102

4 Match the habitats on the left with a definition. Use different colours.

1	grasslands	A	It's very cold here for most of the year, and there's a lot of snow.
2	tropical forests	B	There are very few trees or bushes here, but plenty of space for animals to move around.
3	temperate forests	C	The trees and bushes are very dense, and it's also hot and humid.
4	polar regions	D	There are lots of trees here, and the weather is never too hot or too cold.

5 Write the correct animal.

~~penguin~~	arctic wolf	hedgehog
red deer	polar bear	orangutan
kangaroo	red squirrel	giraffe

1 I'm a bird, but I can't fly. __penguin__

2 I've got big back legs and I move around by jumping. _____

3 I'm small and brown, and I've got thin, sharp parts all over my body.

   _____

4 I use my long neck to reach up and eat leaves on the trees. _____

5 I'm a big, strong animal with thick, white fur and I live at the North Pole.

   _____ _____

6 I'm small, I live in trees and I've got a thick tail. _____ _____

7 I look like a big monkey, and I've got red fur. _____

8 I eat grass and live in large groups. I can run fast. _____ _____

9 I live in very cold areas, and you can often hear me calling at night.

   _____ _____

Need help? ➔ **Student's Book** page 106

We use adjectives ending in **-ed** to describe **how we feel**.
When we add **-ed** to a verb that ends in a consonant + y, the y changes to i:
worry ➔ worried.

We use adjectives ending in **-ing** to describe **the thing that makes us feel like that**.

When we add **-ed** or **-ing** to a verb that ends in a consonant + e, the e is dropped.
e.g. **challenge ➔ challenged ➔ challenging**

---

6 Complete the adjectives with -ed or -ing.

Rainforest adventure!

Do you want a challeng**ing** holiday this year? Why not come on a rainforest adventure! You definitely won't be disappoint**ed** ! You'll see some amaz____ animals, and experience one of the most excit____ places on Earth! You don't need to feel worri____ about dangers, because the trip is carefully planned with safety in mind, and it ends with a relax____ few days in a luxury hotel. Visit our website today for more details – you'll be surpris____ how low our prices are!

Need help? ➔ **Student's Book** page 104

GRAMMAR

Scan the QR code and watch
the grammar animation.

When we feel sure that something is true or
isn't true, we use **must** or **can't**.

When we think something is possible or isn't
possible but we aren't sure, we use **might**,
may or **could** and **might not** or **may not**.

We don't use mustn't, can or couldn't when
we are speculating.

1 Circle the correct modals of speculation.

Hi Jo,

This is day five of my jungle adventure,
and we're staying in a small hotel tonight
– luxury! It's really hot, and there are dark
clouds so I think it (could) / must rain again
soon. We can hear lots of monkeys in the
jungle, but our guide says we could / (may)
(not) see them because they stay high up
in the trees. There are also lots of snakes,
and I'm sure some of them can / must be
poisonous, which is a bit scary. We keep
seeing things moving in the river. Freddie
says they can't / mustn't be crocodiles
because there aren't any in this region, but
I still think I can / may stay well away from
the water! It can / might be a while before
I can write again because we're going
deeper into the jungle, and I'm sure there
can't / must be wi-fi there!

Take care,
Mia

2 Make the sentences similar in meaning.

(Circle) the correct verb.

1	I'm <u>sure</u> Dan <u>isn't</u> scared of spiders!	Dan (can't) / might be scared of spiders!
2	It's <u>possible that</u> I will go to Africa next summer.	I **can't** / **may** go to Africa next summer.
3	It's <u>possible that</u> we won't see any lions.	We **might not** / **can't** see any lions.

4	<u>Maybe</u> there are sharks in the water.	There **could** / **must** be sharks in the water.
5	It's <u>possible that</u> there aren't any tigers here.	There **may not** / **mustn't** be any tigers here.
6	I'm <u>sure</u> it's difficult living in the Arctic Circle.	It **may** / **must** be difficult living in the Arctic Circle.

For more help, go to the Grammar reference:
→ **Student's Book** page 214

READING

> ✓ **HELPFUL HINT FOR THIS TASK**
>
> - Read the headings (1–4) and <u>underline</u>
>   the coloured words.
>
> - Look at the key words in **bold** in each
>   text A–D.
>
> - Match the coloured words with the key
>   words in the texts. <u>Underline</u> in the
>   same colour.
>
> - Look at the questions 1–6 and match
>   the questions with the key words in
>   each text.

1 **Read the article about wild swimming.**

Look at the statements.

Match the headings with the paragraphs.

1 Wild swimming in the <u>city</u>

2 <u>What is</u> wild swimming?

3 ~~Bored with the swimming pool?~~

4 Is it <u>safe</u>?

A <u>3</u>

There's nothing like the feeling of diving into cool water on a hot summer's day! But for some, **the traditional swimming pool** just **isn't exciting** enough. Instead, they are looking for **something more challenging**, and are turning to wild swimming in increasing numbers.

B __

Wild swimming **simply means swimming in a natural environment**, like the sea, a river or a lake. Fans of the sport say that it is a great way to feel connected with the natural world. They also argue that, although pollution exists, natural water is generally cleaner than that in swimming pools because nothing is added to it, and it isn't full of crowds of people. For the few who are more adventurous, there is the extra challenge of finding more extreme places to test the water, like icy mountain lakes!

C __

It must be exciting to swim in such places, but **there are dangers**, too, and anyone thinking of trying wild swimming should **think carefully about safety**. Many lakes and rivers are very deep. The water may be fast-moving, and it can be difficult to swim against this movement. But even more worrying than this, there could be hidden plants or rubbish under the surface. For this reason, it's a good idea to always walk into the water rather than diving in head first. To help people avoid the dangers, there are several websites which offer advice on **safe places** to swim.

D __

But fortunately, it isn't only in the countryside that people can enjoy a wild swim. Many **big cities have rivers and canals** running through their centres, and some are now opening these to swimmers. In Paris, for example, **people can now swim** in one of the main canals in the city. Swimming wasn't allowed in the canal for nearly a hundred years because of pollution, but in 2017 the government declared that the water was safe and announced official swimming areas with safety officers to make sure there were no accidents. The swimmers soon took advantage of this in their thousands, as it perhaps offers the perfect solution of a wild swimming experience in a safe environment!

2 **Read the article again.**

Write ✓ (true) or ✗ (false).

1 Wild swimming is becoming more popular. _✓_

2 Wild swimmers accept that water in rivers and lakes isn't as clean as the water in swimming pools. ____

3 Most wild swimmers want to enjoy an extreme experience. ____

4 The main danger in rivers and lakes is from fast-moving water. ____

5 People can find safety advice about wild swimming online. ____

6 People have always swum in the canals in Paris. ____

➔ 🎧 **Go to page 104 to read the audioscript.**

> ✅ **HELPFUL HINT FOR THIS TASK**
>
> - Read the questions / sentences before listening.
> - Draw lines between A, B and C.
> - Predict the answer.
> - Think about the words you might hear.
> - Listen and check.

🎧 **13 For each question, (circle) the correct answer.**

You will hear an interview with a man called Rob Tucker, who is an expert on Australian camels.

1 Rob became interested in camels when he

   A read a book about a journey.

   B got a holiday job on a sheep farm.

   C saw a documentary film about camels.

2 Rob says that camels brought to Australia in the 1860s

   A were mainly from Arabian countries.

   B were stronger than camels born in Australia.

   C were accompanied by people who could handle them.

3 Why does Rob think camels were more useful than horses in Australia?

   A They could go for days without drinking water.

   B They could travel over difficult ground.

   C They could walk all day without needing breaks.

4 Why do some Australian farmers today complain about the camels?

   A They damage houses.

   B They break water pipes.

   C They eat the farm animals' food.

5 Rob recommends a camel ride that lasts

   A half a day.

   B one day.

   C three days.

6 Rob says it's sometimes hard to see camels in the wild because

   A they stay away from the roads.

   B their colour is similar to the landscape.

   C the camel population has recently decreased.

For more help with Listening Part 4:
➔ **Student's Book Exam Focus** page 99

PUSH YOURSELF / B2

Complete the words in the sentences.

> hooves   claws   ~~antlers~~   tusks

1 Most kinds of deer have short **tails**. The males use their **a**ntlers for fighting.

2 Elephants can lift almost 350 kilos with their **trunks**. Unfortunately, they are often killed for their **t**_____ .

3 Some horses have long **manes** which can grow down to their knees. Horses are not the only animals that have **h**_____ – sheep, deer and giraffes also have them.

4 Tigers' feet have soft **paws** but very sharp **c**_____ , which can grow to over 10 cm long!

SPEAKING

1 Look at the photo.

Complete the sentences.

middle	~~There's~~	background	left
can see	might	must be	~~This is~~

1 <u>This is</u> a picture of a sports adventure.

2 <u>There's</u> a small beach, which is empty.

3 In the _____ of the picture we _____ a man.

4 He's running along the shore, and it _____ quite cold because he's wearing long trousers and a sweatshirt.

5 On the _____, there's a small object on the ground. I'm not sure what it is.

6 The man is carrying a rucksack. I guess it _____ be to carry some food and drink.

7 In the _____, there are some tall cliffs.

WRITING

1 Cross out the adjective which does NOT fit.

1 There's a small restaurant near the beach which serves **~~relaxing~~** / **delicious** food.

2 You can walk along the **rocky** / **clear** cliffs.

3 It's lovely to swim in the **long** / **cool** water.

4 There are **amazing** / **high** views from the top of the mountain.

5 There are also some very **fresh** / **interesting** towns to visit.

2 Circle the correct linking words.

1 Corsica is an island in the Mediterranean **and** / **but** it's a great place to visit.

2 **Although** / **But** it's quite small, there are lots of things to do.

3 Corsica is a part of France, **because** / **so** people speak French there.

4 There are plenty of beautiful beaches **as well as** / **also** mountains where you can go walking.

5 **What's more** / **Although**, there are lots of hotels which aren't too expensive.

HOW WAS UNIT 8?

Gave it a go ☐

Getting there ☐

Aced it! ☐

9 ALWAYS LEARNING

VOCABULARY

1 **Complete what the student says about school.**

~~Education~~   rules   qualifications
grades   skills

I know that it's important to attend school. Education is important, and it's difficult to get a good job if you don't have _____ . I try to work hard for exams and I usually get good _____ . I know we also learn a lot of useful _____ at school, like planning tasks and working together. The only thing I don't like about school are the _____ !

Need help? → **Student's Book** page 118

2 (Circle) **the correct words.**

1   What's the topic of tomorrow's **degree** / **lecture**? I hope it's something interesting!

2   Did you pass all your exams **last term** / **tutor**? I hope you did!

3   I can't believe that I'll graduate and get my **degree** / **fail** this summer! It's amazing!

4   It's very simple – if you don't revise enough, you'll **fail** / **pass** your exams!

Need help? → **Student's Book** page 120

3 (Circle) **the correct words.**

HOW TO BE A TOP STUDENT

1   It's important to listen carefully in lectures. This will help you to **take** / **do** good notes.

2   Always **do** / **make** homework on time, so you're ready for the next piece of work.

3   Try to **do** / **make** extra research on your own, outside class.

4   If you **do** / **make** a mistake, try to learn from it.

5   Make sure you get enough sleep before you **make** / **take** an exam.

6   Be proud of yourself when you finally **get** / **make** your degree – it's a great achievement!

Need help? → **Student's Book** page 121

GRAMMAR

Scan the QR code and watch the grammar animation.

When we change a sentence from **active** to **passive**, the **object** of the sentence becomes the **subject** of the passive sentence.

Someone **stole my book**. → **My book** was **stolen**.

People **make the cars** in Italy. → **The cars** are **made** in Italy.

We use **be** followed by the past participle of the main verb.

1 Circle the correct words to complete the passive sentences.

1 All students **is** / (**are**) expected to work hard.

2 Our class **is** / **was** cancelled yesterday because the teacher was ill.

3 We **was** / **were** told our exam results yesterday.

4 Lunch **is** / **are** served between 12.30 and 1.30 each day.

5 I think that students now **are** / **were** given too much homework.

6 Spanish **doesn't** / **isn't** taught in all schools in the UK.

2 Complete the passive sentences.

1	Paul and Jamie's parents **sent** them to a private school.	Paul and Jamie <u>were sent</u> to a private school.
2	A famous actress **opened** the new school.	The new school _____ a famous actress.
3	Thousands of young people **enjoy** these summer schools.	These summer schools _____ thousands of young people.

4	The school **spends** a lot of money on new books.	A lot of money _____ on new books.
5	They **don't sell** crisps in the school shop now.	Crisps _____ in the school shop now.
6	The teacher **didn't tell** us about the school trip last week.	We _____ about the school trip last week.

3 Complete the conversations with the correct passive forms of the verbs.

1 **A:** Is this a good college?
  B: Yes. The teachers are good, and everyone (**encourage**) <u>is encouraged</u> to work hard.

2 **A:** Where's your bike?
  B: It (**steal**) _____ yesterday! I'm so annoyed!

3 **A:** How do you usually get your exam results?
  B: They (**send**) _____ by email, or you can look on the college website.

4 **A:** Have we got an exam tomorrow?
  B: Yes! We (**tell**) _____ about it last week!

5 **A:** I was surprised that Dan wasn't at the party on Saturday.
  B: Me too. He (**not invite**) _____ for some reason.

6 **A:** £50 seems cheap for the school trip to London.
  B: Yes, but remember food (**not include**) _____ in that price.

For more help, go to the Grammar reference:
→ **Student's Book** page 215

✓ **HELPFUL HINT FOR THIS TASK**

- Read the questions and highlight the key words.
- Draw lines to separate A, B, C and D.
- Draw lines to separate the paragraphs.
- Use colours for each option to <u>underline</u> key information.

Teacher Jack Greening talks about setting up a school photography club.

Last year the headteacher came and asked me to start a photography club. Our school already has lots of fantastic sports clubs, which is great, but not all students like sport. My classroom's decorated with photos I've taken, but they're not exactly works of art <u>and I wasn't sure I was a good enough photographer to teach others.</u> But I wanted to run a school club and the headteacher promised money for cameras, memory cards, tripods, and so on – so I said yes.

There were so many things to consider before I started, and I knew my colleagues were too busy to help. Should the club be for students with experience? Should it be for the whole school, or only some year-groups? Above all, what did I want to achieve? To enter student competitions, or just to take photos for the school website? In the end I decided my aim was for beginners to have fun with photography. I held the sessions in a science lab where we could lock stuff that we needed for the club in a cupboard.

About fifteen students came to the first session. Some of them were clearly only there to be with their mates. Still, I got them all to take photos of each other. We put these on the screen and the keen students chatted about the good and not so good points. I hadn't expected them to have so many good ideas about what they could do better next time.

The second week, mostly the same students came back, and another twenty-five joined. I had to ask the headteacher to get another teacher to share the sessions. Colleagues heard students talking about the club in lessons and advised me about things to do with students, including taking them to a famous photographer's exhibition. A year later, and I've no regrets about starting this club. The students have worked hard on their photography. Some clearly have a natural ability, which helps. I've already planned next year's photographic projects, but our school cameras are quite basic. To take really amazing photos, the students need a more advanced one of their own – that's the best way to improve.

For each question, (circle) the correct answer.

1 How did Jack feel when he was first asked to set up the photography club?

    A stressed because he had enough to do already

    B worried by the lack of photography equipment

    (C) anxious about his photography skills

    D disappointed as he wanted to run a sports club

2 In the second paragraph, what does Jack say was the most important thing for him to decide?

    A how much help he would need

    B which students the club was for

    C where sessions would take place

    D what the purpose of the club was

3 What surprised Jack at the club's first session?

    A how many different types of students took part

    B how good most of the students' photos were

    C how well students could discuss their photos

    D how serious all the students were about photography

4 How did Jack's colleagues react when they heard about his club?

    A They suggested some possible activities.

    B They offered to run the sessions with Jack.

    C They asked Jack for advice about their own clubs.

    D They recommended some students to join the club.

5 What might Jack say to the parents of students in his photography club?

    A 'I've enjoyed helping your children this year, but in order to make further progress they now need to do a proper photography course.'

    B 'Some of your children had the advantage of previous experience using cameras, but they've all made great progress.'

    C 'If your children are interested in becoming better photographers, encourage them by taking them to see photography exhibitions.'

    D 'To be a great photographer requires talent and lots of practice, but it helps if your children have good cameras too.'

For more help with Reading Part 3:
→ **Student's Book Exam Focus** page 86

→ Go to page 105 to read the audioscript.

> ✓ **HELPFUL HINT FOR THIS TASK**
>
> - Read the questions / sentences before listening.
> - Predict the answer.
> - Think about the words you might hear.
> - Listen and check.

1 🎧 **14 Listen to a radio discussion about learning. Which sentence best summarises the discussion?**

A Stella Bradshaw discusses which new skills are the best ones to learn as an adult.

B Stella Bradshaw talks about the advantages of continuing to learn new things as an adult.

2 🎧 **14 Listen again. Write ✓ (true) or ✗ (false).**

1 Stella wrote her book because of her own experiences.   ✓

2 Mavis Bowman left school because she wasn't keen on learning when she was a teenager.   ____

3 According to Stella, older people don't learn as quickly as younger people.   ____

4 Stella says the main reason for learning new things as an adult is that it makes life more interesting.   ____

5 Kevin learned to ride a bike quite easily when he was 28.   ____

6 Stella's advice to listeners is to avoid things that they found very difficult when they were younger.   ____

PUSH YOURSELF B2

Complete the passive sentences.

1	Someone **has broken** a window in one of the classrooms.	A window in one of the classrooms _has been broken_ .
2	Someone **is repairing** the school minibus at the moment.	The school minibus _____ _____ _____ at the moment.
3	They had announced the winner two weeks earlier.	The winner _____ _____ _____ two weeks earlier.

4	They should clean the classrooms every day.	The classrooms _____ _____ every day.
5	Everyone must complete their project by Friday.	All projects _____ _____ _____ by Friday.
6	You can't use dictionaries in the exam.	Dictionaries _____ _____ _____ in the exam.

WRITING

1 Complete the email with the correct words.

could ~~Dear~~ ~~enquire~~ Finally
know let look sincerely

Dear Mr Green,

I am writing to enquire about the drama course at Homewood Hall.

Please _____ you tell me how long the course lasts? I would also like to _____ if all the equipment is provided.

_____, please could you _____ me know if there are still vacancies on the course?

I _____ forward to hearing from you.

Yours _____,

Emma Ashton

2 Match the direct and indirect questions. Use different colours.

1	Where does the course **take place?**	A	Please let me know what I should **bring** with me.
2	Is **food included** in the price?	B	I'd like to know where the course **takes place.**
3	What should I **bring** with me?	C	Please could you tell me if **food is included** in the price?
4	Can I get to the **college by bus?**	D	Please could you tell me if I can get to the **college by bus?**

SPEAKING

1 Match the sentence halves about likes and dislikes at school. Use different colours.

1	I love	A	at maths.
2	I'm not very interested	B	in history.
3	When I was younger, I was quite good	C	chemistry and biology.

4	I'm bored	D	on English.
5	I can't	E	by physics.
6	I'm quite keen	F	stand economics!

2 Complete the sentences with the correct words.

~~don't~~ find thought by at can't

1 I _don't_ mind biology, but I hate physics!

2 I've always been terrible _____ art.

3 I really don't like history. I _____ it really dull!

4 I'm fascinated _____ different countries, so I love geography.

5 I _____ bear IT – it's my worst subject!

6 When I was younger, I _____ maths was boring, but now I know how important it is.

HOW WAS UNIT 9?

Gave it a go ☐

Getting there ☐

Aced it! ☐

10 TRAVELLING WELL

VOCABULARY

1 Complete the words in the sentences.

~~port~~ ferry   traffic jam   flight
platform   delay   petrol station

1   the place where **boats** arrive and leave from: p<u>ort</u>

2   a **large boat** that carries **passengers** and sometimes **cars**: f_____

3   a situation when the **cars** and **lorries** on the road **cannot move** forwards: t____ j_____

4   a journey by **plane**: f_____

5   the place where a **train** leaves from at a **railway station**: p_____

6   a situation when **trains**, **buses** or **planes** are **late**: d_____

7   a **place** where you can buy **fuel** for your car: p_____ s_____

Need help? ➔ **Student's Book** page 128

2 Complete the advice about flying with the correct words.

departure lounge   airline   check-in
~~business class~~   cabin staff   gate
flight attendant

Tips for stress-free flying

1   When you buy your ticket, think about paying a bit more for a <u>business class</u> seat – they're a lot more comfortable!

2   Make sure you know which _____ you are travelling with before you get to the airport.

3   When you get to the airport, go straight to _____ to collect your boarding pass.

4   Wait in the _____ _____ until your plane is ready to board.

5   When your plane is ready to board, go to the correct _____.

6   The _____ _____ will greet you as you get on the plane.

7   If you have any problems during your flight, speak to a _____ _____.

Need help? ➔ **Student's Book** page 129

GRAMMAR

Scan the QR code and watch the grammar animation.

1 Complete the zero conditional sentences with the correct form of the verbs.

1 **If** the weather **(be)** _is_ bad, I usually **(get)** _get_ the bus to college.

2 **When** I **(go)** _____ on holiday, I **(prefer)** _____ to travel by plane.

3 Everyone **(complain)** _____ **if** the train **(be)** _____ late.

4 I always **(feel)** _____ better **when** I **(walk)** _____ to work.

5 You **(save)** _____ a lot of money **if** you **(use)** _____ your bike to get around the city.

6 **If** you **(buy)** _____ your tickets in advance, they **(be)** _____ much cheaper.

2 Complete the first conditional sentences with the correct form of the verbs.

1 It's raining! We **(get)** _'ll get_ wet **if** we **(walk)** _walk_ !

2 What **(we / do)** _____ **if** Jack **(not / be)** _____ at the airport to meet us?

3 You need to hurry up. You **(miss)** _____ your plane **unless** you **(leave)** _____ now!

4 **If** you **(pay)** _____ for the coffees, I **(buy)** _____ you a sandwich on the flight!

5 I **(go)** _____ to Oxford by car, **unless** the roads **(be)** _____ too busy.

6 **If** the bus **(be)** _____ late, we **(get)** _____ a taxi.

3 Make the sentences similar in meaning.

(Circle) the correct verb.

1	We'll only go to the beach if it's sunny.	We (won't go) / don't go to the beach unless (it's) / it will be sunny.
2	We'll go to the concert unless the tickets are too expensive.	We won't go / don't go to the concert if the tickets are / will be too expensive.
3	If I pass all my exams, my parents will buy me a new phone.	My parents won't buy / don't buy me a new phone unless I pass / will pass all my exams.
4	We won't get a taxi unless there are no buses.	We'll only get / We only get a taxi if there will be / are no buses.
5	I'll buy some shoes if I see some that I like.	I don't buy / won't buy any shoes unless I see / will see some that I like.

PUSH YOURSELF / B2

🔊 15 **Listen to four people talking about cycle paths.** (Circle) **the correct opinion for each person.**

1 A They're quite dangerous.
  (B) They're good, and safe to use.

2 A You can easily see where you're going.
  B They're difficult to follow.

3 A They aren't good at all.
  B There should be more of them.

4 A There aren't enough of them.
  B They're sometimes too crowded.

4 Complete the sentences with correct verb forms. Use the zero or first conditional.

1 I always **(walk)** walk through the park **when** it **(be)** is sunny.

2 I **(call)** _____ you from the station later **if** there **(be)** _____ any delays with the trains.

3 If I **(see)** _____ Rob this afternoon, I **(tell)** _____ him you're looking for him.

4 Tara always **(get)** _____ annoyed if the bus **(be)** _____ late!

5 If I **(go)** _____ to work early, there **(be)** _____ always plenty of seats on the train.

5 Complete the text with the correct second conditional form of the verbs.

```
●●● ◁▷                    🔍 🏠
```

Should we simply stop using plastic?

A lot of people think the world **(be)** would be a better place if we **(stop)** stopped using plastic. But is it really that simple? For example, if we **(use)** used glass bottles for things like milk, they **(be)** would be heavier. If lorries **(have to)** _____ carry more weight, they **(use)** _____ more fuel, and this **(cause)** _____ more pollution. Also, if we **(not / have)** _____ plastic for things like bags and phone cases, companies **(make)** _____ more things out of leather, so we **(have)** _____ more animals, and they **(need)** _____ more water and food.

A lot of clothes use plastic too, and if we **(change)** _____ to more natural materials, we **(grow)** _____ more cotton and we **(keep)** _____ more sheep for wool — all using more energy! As you can see, the problem of plastic is simple, but the solutions are much more difficult!

6 Complete the sentences with the correct verb forms.

1 If I **(have)** had lots of money, I **(travel)** would travel all around the world!

2 Our old car never **(start)** starts easily **when** the weather **(be)** is cold.

3 I'll go for a pizza with you on Saturday if I **(have)** have enough money.

4 **If** I **(eat)** _____ chocolate, it **gives** me a headache.

5 **If** the trains **were** more comfortable, more people **(use)** _____ them.

6 **If** you **tell** me what time your train arrives tomorrow, I **(come)** _____ to the station to meet you.

7 I'll **ride** my bike to college tomorrow **unless** I **(have)** _____ a lot of books to carry.

8 You **would be** much fitter **if** you **(walk)** _____ to work every day!

For more help, go to the Grammar reference:
→ **Student's Book** pages 216–217

READING

1 Read the article. Which <u>sentence</u> best <u>sums up</u> what the <u>article</u> says?

A Plastic rubbish on beaches isn't a big problem yet, but it will be in a few years.

B Plastic rubbish on beaches is a big problem, but people are finding creative solutions.

C The problem of plastic rubbish on beaches is getting worse, and the government should do something about it.

2 Read the article again. Which project are the sentences about? Write V (volunteer), A (art) or K (kayak).

1 They <u>sort</u> the <u>rubbish</u> that they <u>collect</u>. V

2 The project receives money to pay for the work. ___

3 They give the things that they make to local people. ___

4 They enjoy the work that they do. ___

5 They try to persuade other people to join in and help. ___

6 They sell the things that they make. ___

A sea of plastic

A recent storm in the south west of England brought an unexpected problem – large amounts of plastic rubbish on the beaches. The oceans are full of plastic, and when a storm moves the water more than usual, it can also lift this rubbish from the bottom of the sea and move it to the shore. It is clearly a big problem, but some people are now taking action themselves.

The power of volunteers

In one town, a group of local people have decided to clean up their beach themselves. Although they are all volunteers, so they aren't paid, they spend every weekend down on the shore, collecting as much rubbish as they can. **They put it into different bags, depending on the type.** They sell anything valuable, recycle as much as possible, and leave the rest to be taken away as rubbish. They also **encourage tourists who use the beach to pick up five pieces of rubbish** before they leave.

From rubbish to art

One family is using art to make people think about the problem of plastic in the oceans. Sara and John Bailey, together with their two children, regularly collect rubbish from the beach near their home and use it to create works of art. Sara says **they have great fun** together choosing which things to use and thinking of clever ways to use them. **The works of art go into local shops**, and the money they make from them pays for any materials that they need.

Boats to collect more rubbish

A bigger project is using plastic from the oceans to create useful products for local people. The project, which **receives financial help** from the government, collects plastic from the beach. It sends it to a local factory, where it is recycled and made into kayaks, or small boats. These **kayaks go back to local people at no cost**, and people can then use them to spend time on the sea collecting more plastic.

Although governments clearly need to take action to deal with the problem of plastic in the oceans, it seems that individuals and local groups can also be a big part of the solution.

LISTENING PART 2

→ 🔊 **Go to page 106 to read the audioscript.**

> ✅ **HELPFUL HINT FOR THIS TASK**
>
> - Read the questions before listening.
> - Predict the answer.
> - Think about the words you might hear.
> - Listen and check.

🔊 **16 For each question, (circle) the correct answer.**

1 You will hear two friends talking about a new airport.

They both think that

A the location is very convenient.

(B) the recycling facilities are great.

C the signs are extremely clear.

2 You will hear a woman telling her brother about her new electric bicycle.

How does she feel about it?

A not sure about how long it will last

B worried about where to leave it at college

C embarrassed about going to college on it

3 You will hear two colleagues talking about travelling to work.

Why does the man prefer taking the train?

A He can do some work before arriving at his office.

B There's nowhere to park near where he works.

C It takes too long to get home in the evenings.

4 You will hear two friends talking about getting to the airport.

They agree to

A make a decision after doing some research.

B travel to the airport together.

C wait for each other at the entrance.

5 You will hear two neighbours talking about traffic in the town.

The man thinks that

A the roads are confusing for visitors.

B fewer cars are already coming into the town.

C more changes are needed to solve the problems.

6 You will hear two friends talking about recycling.

The woman says that she

A uses more glass than plastic.

B finds it hard to avoid using plastic.

C is careful which types of plastic she uses.

For more help with Listening Part 2:
→ **Student's Book Exam Focus** page 34

SPEAKING

1 **Read the sentences.**

Circle **the correct meaning for each sentence.**

1 **I think** the two boys must be brothers.

   A **I'm sure** they are brothers.

   B **It's possible** that they are brothers.

2 They **might** be on holiday.

   A **I'm sure** they are on holiday.

   B **It's possible** that they are on holiday.

3 It **may** not be her car.

   A **I'm sure** it isn't her car.

   B **It's possible** that it isn't her car.

4 It **can't** be summer.

   A **It's possible** that it's not summer.

   B **I'm sure** it isn't summer.

5 It **could** be some kind of meat.

   A **It's possible** that it's some kind of meat.

   B **I'm sure** it's some kind of meat.

2 **Match sentences with similar meanings. Use different colours.**

1	I'm sure it's a rescue boat.	A	She can't be very old.
2	I guess it's possible that he's a teacher.	B	It must be a rescue boat.
3	I'm sure she isn't very old.	C	I guess he could be a teacher.

WRITING

1 **Circle** **the correct narrative tenses.**

Last Thursday evening, I **had sat /
was sitting** in the Top Pizza restaurant
on West Street, waiting for some friends.
The waiter **came / was coming** over
and asked if I wanted to order. 'No, not
yet,' I **replied / was replying**. I **looked /
was looking** at the time on my phone. It
was 7.45. Where were they? We **agreed
/ had agreed** to meet at 7.30. While I
thought / was thinking about what to
do next, my phone **rang / was ringing**.
'Where are you?' my friend Callum
asked / had asked. 'We're all waiting
for you in the Top Pizza restaurant on
Bridge Street!'

2 **Rewrite the direct speech with the correct punctuation.**

1 nice to meet you she said

   'Nice to meet you,' she said.

2 where are you going he asked

   _____

3 **Circle** **the correct verbs.**

1 'Don't make too much noise,' he
   whispered / **cried**.

2 'Are you feeling better?' she **asked /
said**.

3 'Hello!' he **told / called**.

4 'You can't come in!' I **asked / shouted**.

HOW WAS UNIT 10?

Gave it a go   ☐

Getting there   ☐

Aced it!   ☐

11 A GREAT LOCATION

VOCABULARY

1 Complete the people's descriptions of their homes.

| cosy | ~~terraced house~~ | old-fashioned |

> I live in a <u>terraced</u> <u>house</u> near the city centre. It's quite small, but it's warm and _____ . It's an _____-_____ house, not a modern one, but I like it!

| suburbs | convenient | two-storey |

> I live in quite a big house in the _____ , about five miles from the city centre. It's a _____-_____ house, with an upstairs and a downstairs. It's a brand new house, so everything in it is very modern. It's quite close to my school, which is very _____ .

| district | floor | flats |

> I live in a tall block of _____ in the city centre, near the business _____ where my dad works. We live on the top _____ , so we have a great view of the city!

Need help? ➔ **Student's Book** page 140

2 Choose the correct answer.

1   Where can you heat water?
   Ⓐ a kettle   **B** a tap

2   Where do you hang clothes?
   A a desk   **B** a wardrobe

3   What do you put on your bed?
   A a rug   **B** a duvet

4   Where do you put rubbish?
   A a rug   **B** a bin

5   Where can you get water from?
   A a bin   **B** a tap

6   What do you put on the floor?
   A a rug   **B** a cushion

7   Where can you keep things in a bathroom?
   A a cabinet   **B** a bin

3 Complete the sentences.

| sink   heating   ~~cabinet~~   cushions wardrobe   rug |

1   The mirror on the bathroom <u>cabinet</u> is cracked.

2   The _____ isn't working properly, so the flat is cold.

3   There's a horrible stain on the _____ on the hall floor.

4   The _____ from the sofa are missing.

5   One _____ and one chest of drawers aren't enough for two people.

6   The tap on the kitchen _____ needs fixing. We can't turn it off.

Need help? ➔ **Student's Book** page 143

GRAMMAR

Scan the QR code and watch the grammar animation.

In **relative clauses** we use:

Which and that for **things**.

Who and that for **people**.

When for **time/s**.

Where for **places**.

Whose for **possessions** or **relationships**.

Relative clauses which are **essential** for the **meaning** of the sentence are called **defining relative clauses**.

Relative clauses which just **add extra information** and can be removed without changing the meaning are called **non-defining relative clauses**.

1 (Circle) the correct relative pronouns.

1 Jan showed me the house **which** / **where** she lives.

2 The people **that** / **whose** I share a flat with are all really friendly.

3 This is the flat **which** / **who** they want to buy.

4 The friend **who** / **whose** house I stayed at is called Eva.

5 The people **who** / **which** live next door to us are very nice.

6 This was a time **when** / **which** most people lived together in big family groups.

7 The sofa **that** / **who** we bought was too big for the room.

2 Complete with who or which.

1 Some of the houses _which_ we looked at were too expensive for us to rent.

2 The person _____ owns our flat also owns five other flats.

3 My friend Tom, _____ lives in London, is mad about skateboarding.

4 Our flat, _____ is near the city centre, is quite small and modern.

5 It takes me nearly an hour to get to school, _____ is annoying.

3 Look at the relative clauses in exercise 2 again.

In which two sentences can you use that instead of which or who? Write ✓ (true) or ✗ (false).

1 ____✓____   4 _____

2 _____   5 _____

3 _____

4 Read the blog post. Underline three bold relative pronouns that you can leave out.

This is the first week in my new flat, and I love it! For a start, it's close to a big park, **which** is great! It's also close to the school **where** I'll go in September. And my friend Sam, **who** I've known all my life, lives just around the corner. What could be better? The bedroom **that** I've chosen is quite big. All the things **which** I brought with me from our old flat fit in easily. The other people **who** live on our floor also seem very nice. One boy **who** I've met likes the same computer games as me, so I'm sure we'll be friends!

5 **Join the sentences. Add a relative pronoun.**

1	This is the **swimming pool**. I use it in the summer.	This is the swimming pool _which_ I use in the summer.
2	The **new flats** are expensive. They are building them in the business district.	The flats _____ they are building in the business district are expensive.
3	**My friend Sam** lives in the suburbs. He's really sporty.	My friend Sam, _____ is really sporty, lives in the suburbs.

4	**Manchester** is a great city. I live there.	Manchester, _____ I live, is a great city.
5	You can use these **tennis courts** for free. It's amazing!	You can use these tennis courts for free, _____ is amazing!
6	I have met some **new friends**. They are all very nice.	The new friends _____ I have met are all very nice.

When we talk about arranging for another person to do a job for us we can use these constructions:

Have/get + object + past participle

I had/got a photo taken when I graduated from university.

Have is more formal than **get**.

6 **Complete the sentences. Use the correct form of get or have.**

1	**Someone took** our photo next to the fountain.	We **(have)** _had_ our photo taken next to the fountain.
2	**I need to ask someone** to fix my phone this weekend.	I need **(get)** _____ my phone fixed this weekend.
3	Has **someone cut** your hair?	Have you **(have)** _____ your hair cut?

4	You **can ask someone** to deliver your groceries to your home.	You can **(have)** _____ your groceries delivered to your home.
5	You **can ask someone to check** your running style before you buy new trainers.	It's a good idea to **(get)** _____ your running style checked before you buy new trainers.

For more help, go to the Grammar reference:
→ **Student's Book** pages 217–218

LISTENING

→ 🎧 Go to page 108 to read the audioscript.

> ✓ **HELPFUL HINT FOR THIS TASK**
>
> - Read the questions and <u>underline</u> the key words.
> - Listen and highlight the key words in different colours when the speakers mention them.
> - Remember you listen twice.

1 🎧 **17 Listen to three young people talking about where they live in London. What have they all found?**

A a clever way to meet new people and make friends

B an unusual way to live cheaply in the city

2 🎧 **17 Listen again. Which person, Ewan, Daisy, or Andy ...**

1 has met other young people that they have something in common with?
   Andy

2 doesn't have a very good bathroom?
   _____

3 had some problems when they first moved into their home? _____

4 is free to make changes to their home?
   _____

5 is going to leave their home soon?
   _____

6 lives close to their job? _____

PUSH YOURSELF B2

Complete the advertisements for flats to rent with adjectives.

> furnished ~~stunning~~ unique
> ~~residential~~ picturesque delightful
> luxurious spacious

For rent
A double room in a **s**<u>tunning</u> modern flat in a quiet **r**<u>esidential</u> area. The room is fully **f**_____, and all bills are included in the rent.

For rent
A **d**_____ two-bedroom flat in the city centre. Very **s**_____, and with a large balcony.

For rent
A **u**_____ three-bedroom flat in the business district. It has a **l**_____ modern bathroom and **p**_____ views over the city.

> ✅ **HELPFUL HINT FOR THIS TASK**
>
> - Draw lines to separate questions 1–6.
> - Circle 1, 2, etc. in a different colour.
> - Highlight the words before and after the gap.

For each question, circle the correct answer.

Houses that can turn around

Would you like to live in a house that follows the direction of the sun in winter and provides shade when it's really hot? This is fast becoming a **(1)** _____C_____ , as more architects around the world are designing buildings that turn around. Known as 'rotating houses', these homes are the **(2)** _____ solution for anyone who's ever **(3)** _____ like waking up to a different view from their bedroom window. And many of these houses are controlled by motors no bigger than **(4)** _____ washing machines.

Luke Everingham lives in a rotating house built with glass, metal and natural **(5)** _____ such as wood. The house is an eight-sided shape and there are eight rooms inside. Luke uses a remote control in the living room to make his house turn. It takes thirty minutes to complete a full circle, so you can't **(6)** _____ it's turning unless you focus on an object outside.

1 A fact	**B** truth	**C** reality	**D** habit
2 A great	**B** perfect	**C** good	**D** fantastic
3 A thought	**B** dreamt	**C** wanted	**D** felt
4 A ordinary	**B** frequent	**C** usual	**D** casual
5 A materials	**B** ingredients	**C** contents	**D** parts
6 A find	**B** compare	**C** tell	**D** learn

For more help with Reading Part 5:
➔ **Student's Book Exam Focus** page 98

WRITING

1 Circle the correct words.

1 Thank you **of** / **for** your email.

2 Congratulations **on** / **for** your exam results.

3 I'm **afraid** / **scared** I can't come to the party.

4 Perhaps I **would** / **could** visit you in July?

5 I'm looking forward to **see** / **seeing** you soon.

6 Write **back** / **me** soon.

2 Complete the email with the correct words.

unfortunately   ~~Dear~~   looking
Perhaps   getting   best

Dear Matt,

Thank you for your email. Congratulations on _____ a place at college!

Thank you for inviting me to your party. I'd love to come, but _____ I can't. I will be at my grandma's house that week.

_____ we could meet when I get back, and do something together?

I'm really _____ forward to seeing you soon and hearing all about your plans.

All the _____ ,

Sam

SPEAKING

1 Match the halves of the expressions. Use different colours

1	No	A	joking!
2	How	B	way!
3	You're	C	That's unbelievable!
4	Wow!	D	incredible!

2 Circle the correct words to complete the description.

We're staying in an amazing holiday flat, right by the beach. There's one big room for living in and there's, **kind** / **like**, a big glass door which opens out onto a **types of** / **kind of** large balcony, where you can sit and see the sea. There's a big games room, with a table tennis table and **stuff** / **sorts** like that. There's **a type of** / **a kind** outdoor cooker where you can barbecue and cook your meals outside. And there's a shed outside with things for the beach – surfboards, small boats, those **stuff** / **kinds** of things. Down by the beach, there's **kind** / **a sort** of natural swimming pool in the rocks, where the water's really warm – perfect!

HOW WAS UNIT 11?

Gave it a go

Getting there

Aced it!

12 THE PERFECT JOB

VOCABULARY

1 Read the clues and write the jobs.

> ~~plumber~~ electrician lawyer
> pharmacist accountant

1 'Call me if you have a problem with your taps.' <u>plumber</u>

2 'I'm good at maths, and you can trust me with your money!' _____

3 'I help people when they have to go to court.' _____

4 'You can come to me if you're ill and need medicines or tablets.' _____

5 'Call me if the lights in your house suddenly go out!' _____

2 Choose the best job.

> politician architect lecturer
> ~~programmer~~ astronaut

1 'I think computers are amazing – and you can make them do some really cool things.' <u>programmer</u>

2 'I enjoy teaching, but I'd like to teach older students.' _____

3 'I think there are a lot of problems in the world today, and I'd like to do something to help.' _____

4 'I want to see the world – from as far away as possible!' _____

5 'I love buildings, especially modern ones.' _____

Need help? → **Student's Book** page 160

3 Circle the correct adjectives.

1 Maria **never gets angry**, even if she has to show me how to do something three times! **creative** / (**patient**)

2 Dan comes up with some amazing **new ideas**! **creative** / **flexible**

3 Rob is really good at solving problems – he's so **clever**! **intelligent** / **friendly**

4 Abi **never** seems **stressed**, even when we're really busy. **calm** / **creative**

5 Ollie **always** says **hello** to other people, and asks how they are. **flexible** / **friendly**

4 Complete the tips with the correct words.

> ~~co-workers~~ employee line manager
> director

How to be happy and successful at work

1 Be cheerful and polite to the people you work with – your <u>co-workers</u> don't want to work with someone who's always complaining!

2 If you have any problems, the first person to talk to is your _____ _____ – this is the person who is directly above you in the company.

3 Remember you are part of a team at work – you aren't the only _____ in the company!

4 If you are ambitious, be patient – it takes about twenty years to reach the top and become the _____ of a company!

Need help? → **Student's Book** page 154

5 **Complete the information on a careers website with the correct words.**

| good with | problem-solving | ~~certificate~~ |

Being a plumber is a great job if you like working with your hands. You can start a training course straight after high school, and at the end you will get a _certificate_ to show you are able to do the job. You must be friendly and _____ _____ people, and sometimes you have to work out the best way to do something, so you need _____ _____ skills.

| doctorate | ~~master's~~ | good at communication |

To become a university lecturer, you need a bachelor's degree and a _master's_ degree, and finally, you have to spend three more years at university studying for a _____. Apart from these qualifications, you also need to be _____ _____ presenting information, and of course you also need excellent _____ skills so you can explain your ideas to students.

Need help? → **Student's Book pages 157 and 160**

GRAMMAR

Scan the QR code and watch the grammar animation.

1 (Circle) **the correct modal verbs.**

1 A: (Could) / **Must** I borrow your pen, please?
   B: Yes, of course you **could** / (can).

2 A: **May** / **Couldn't** I speak to Chris, please?
   B: No, I'm sorry, you **can't** / **couldn't** speak to him. He's in a meeting.

3 A: **Must** / **Can** I eat my lunch at my desk?
   B: Yes, that's fine, but you **couldn't** / **mustn't** spill food on your laptop!

4 A: **Are we allowed to** / **Must we** finish early on a Friday?
   B: Yes, but you **couldn't** / **can't** leave before 4 p.m.

2 **Read the school rules from 1900. Complete the sentences with the correct form of** **had to** **or** **be allowed to.**

- All children must be in school by 8.30 a.m.

- Uniform is black skirts for girls and short trousers for boys under 11, long trousers for boys over 11.

- Coats may be kept on in cold weather.

In 1900, the children _had to_ be in school by 8.30 a.m. Boys under 11 years old _____ wear short trousers. Girls _____ wear black skirts. They _____ keep their coats on in the classroom in cold weather.

3 Circle the correct answer.

1   My parents usually let me stay up late at the weekend.
   A   I can't stay up late at the weekend.
   (B)   I am allowed to stay up late at the weekend.

2   My parents make me do my homework before I can play on the computer.
   A   I have to do my homework first.
   B   I am not allowed to do my homework first.

3   My brother didn't let me borrow his bike last weekend.
   A   I was allowed to borrow his bike.
   B   I wasn't allowed to borrow his bike.

4   When I was younger, my parents made me help around the house.
   A   I was allowed to help around the house.
   B   I had to help around the house.

4 Complete the sentence so it has a similar meaning. Use the words.

1	My parents say I **have to keep** my bedroom tidy.	My parents **(make)** _make_ me keep my bedroom tidy.
2	Our teachers say we **can't use** our phones in class.	Our teachers **(not let)** _____ _____ us use our phones in class.
3	Her boss **didn't let** her go home early.	She **(not allow)** _____ _____ to go home early.
4	Mum **made me go** to bed early.	I **(have)** _____ to go to bed early.
5	Our teacher says we're **allowed to** look online.	Our teacher **(let)** _____ us look online.

For more help, go to the Grammar reference:
➜ **Student's Book** page 219

READING

1 **Match the jobs with the meanings.**

1	farmer	**A**	someone who cooks food in a restaurant
2	chef	**B**	someone who uses a <u>machine</u> to serve <u>coffee</u> in a <u>café</u>
3	barista	**C**	someone who looks after young children while their parents are working
4	childcare assistant	**D**	someone who grows crops and keeps animals to produce food

---

✔ **HELPFUL HINT FOR THIS TASK**

- Read the job descriptions above again.
- <u>Underline</u> the key words in each paragraph.
- <u>Underline</u> words in the job descriptions above which match key words in the paragraphs.

---

2 **Read the article. Match the correct job with each paragraph.**

A   ~~pharmacist~~

B   childcare assistant

C   farmer

D   chef

E   barista

F   tour guide

3 **Read the statements.**

Read the article again.

Which job is each sentence about?

1 There are plans to do more work using robots in the future. _farmer_

2 Robots don't get tired. _____

3 Customers want a real person to help them gain more from an experience. _____

4 This robot hasn't made a mistake yet. _____

5 Robots can't do this job because they don't have all the senses that humans have. _____

6 Robots can't do this job because they don't understand how people are feeling. _____

ARE ROBOTS TAKING OUR JOBS?

Some people worry that robots will carry out a lot more of our jobs in the future. But is this true? Which jobs can robots do, and which jobs will they never be able to do?

1 _____

In some cafés, coffee is already served by a robot, or a robot arm at least. The arm picks up a cup, moves it to the coffee machine and presses the buttons to produce a perfect cup of coffee in about 30 seconds, which is faster than a human. **Another advantage is the robot never needs a break**, and it doesn't get angry with difficult customers!

2 _____

On the other hand, if you go into a restaurant kitchen, you will find the staff are still one hundred percent human. Cooking is a creative activity, and no one has managed to produce a creative robot yet. Experts also believe that robots will never be able to cook delicious food because **they can't smell or taste it.**

3 _A Pharmacist_

At one university in the United States, there is already a robot which prepares medicines for patients to collect. Doctors order the medicines online, then the robot puts the correct tablets into bottles and prints the labels. **So far, the robot hasn't got anything wrong**, and it is better than a human pharmacist because it can check more easily whether two medicines might not work well together.

4 _____

Robots can teach some things such as languages, but experts say **they will never be able to look after young children**. Young children need human contact, and they need people who can understand them. Robots can be taught to recognise behaviours, such as when someone laughs or gets angry, but they will never know when someone is upset or lonely, or scared.

5 _____

The job of growing food includes a lot of routine work which robots can definitely do. This year, a British university has completed a project to grow a complete crop hands-free, using only machines to plant it, look after it, and pick it. **They now want to work towards running a whole farm using just machines.**

6 _____

We now spend more and more of our working and home lives with machines. Research shows that when we're on holiday, however, we want more human contact. **People who know a place well can help us to enjoy new places and new adventures** in a way that is exciting and challenging for us. For this reason, humans will always be needed for this job.

➜ 🔊 Go to page 108 to read the audioscript.

> ✅ **HELPFUL HINT FOR THIS TASK**
>
> - Read the questions and highlight key words.
> - Look at the pictures. Write any words you know.
> - Listen for the answer to the question.

🔊 18 **For each question, ⃝circle the correct answer.**

1 What is the woman's job now?

Ⓐ   B   C

2 Which benefit does the man's company offer staff?

A   B   C

3 Who works in the sales department?

A   B   C

4 Where does the man work?

A   B   C

5 What does the woman like best about her job?

A   B   C

6 What was the man's career ambition when he was a child?

A   B   C

7 Who is the woman's sister?

A   B   C

For more help with Listening Part 1:
➜ **Student's Book Exam Focus** page 60

PUSH YOURSELF B2

Match the sentences with similar meanings.

1	He's right there, on the other side of the room. I'm sure you can **see him**!	**A**	We may / might be able to **buy our uniforms** online.
2	It will be possible for you to **talk to her** tomorrow.	**B**	You must be able **to see him**.
3	It's possible that we can **buy our uniforms** online.	**C**	You will be able to **talk to her** tomorrow.

SPEAKING

1 Circle the correct words.

1 A: I think that politicians should be paid more.

   B: **Sorry, but** / Yes, but I don't agree.

2 A: We need to encourage more people to become teachers.

   B: Really? / **Exactly!** We really need more teachers.

3 A: Nurses should get the same salary as doctors.

   B: I'm afraid **I disagree** / I'm sorry.

4 A: Firefighters do a dangerous job.

   B: Yes, you're **right** / kind.

2 Circle the correct expression.

1 A: I think George would be a brilliant politician!

   B: Sorry, but I don't agree. / (Yes, you're right.) He really wants to make people's lives better.

2 A: I think working as a programmer would be fun.

   B: Exactly! / **I don't think that's true.** I think a lot of their work is really quite boring!

3 A: It's easy to become an electrician!

   B: I agree with you. / **I'm afraid I disagree.** You have to do a lot of training.

WRITING

Complete the job advertisement.

> qualifications Applicants full-time must ~~opportunity~~ application should be able

Why not become a **magic assistant**? This is a great _opportunity_ for someone who enjoys being on the stage! This is a _____-_____ job, starting next month.

_____ should be 18 years old. They _____ _____ _____ to make decisions quickly and keep smiling when things go wrong. They _____ be brave and able to hide their fear! There are no _____ necessary for this job – we will consider anyone who loves magic shows!

Please send your _____ to jojomagic@magicshows.org.

HOW WAS UNIT 12?

Gave it a go ☐

Getting there ☐

Aced it! ☐

13 GET INVOLVED!

VOCABULARY

1 Complete what the people say about sport with the verbs.

| represent | joined | take up |

I decided last year that I should <u>take up</u> a new sport, so I _____ my local tennis club. I love it! I'm much healthier now and I even _____ the club in matches from time to time!

| beat | take part | going out |

I do athletics, but just for fun. I don't often _____ _____ in competitions. I don't want to take it too seriously because I also enjoy _____ _____ at the weekend. It's fun when I _____ my friends in races, though!

| scored | support | held |

I love football! I _____ my local team and I go to all their games. Last year, the club _____ a competition to find the most loyal fan, and I was in the top ten! I sometimes play football with my friends, but I've never _____ a goal!

Need help? → **Student's Book** page 166

2 Read the definitions and write the words.

| referee   opponents   ~~competitor~~
teammates   supporters |

1 someone who takes part in a competition: <u>competitor</u>

2 the people you play against in a sport: _____

3 people who watch a team and want them to win: _____

4 the people you play in a game or competition with: _____

5 the person who decides if the players are following the rules in a game: _____

Need help? → **Student's Book** page 167

3 Circle the correct words.

What's your sporting dream?

I'd like to **do** / **go** running in the desert!
Emma, 16

I'd like to be fit enough to climb a mountain and then **play** / **do** a workout at the top!
Erica, 15

I want to **play** / **go** ice skating on a frozen lake in Canada – cool! Stella, 16

I'd love to **do** / **play** basketball with one of the great American teams! Paul, 15

I'd like to **play** / **do** yoga on an empty beach in the Caribbean! Rose, 15

4 Complete the quiz with the correct words.

Then do the quiz and check your score.

pitch   court   ~~rink~~   pool
ramp   course   track

Sports trivia – test your knowledge!

1 The biggest natural ice skating __rink__ is the Rideau Canal in **Canada / Russia**. It is 7.8 km long.

2 The most footballs on a football _____ is over **50,000 / 150,000**!

3 The deepest swimming _____ is in Italy and is **32 / 42** metres deep. It is used for diving.

4 The oldest ball boy to collect balls on a tennis _____ during an official match was the American Manny Hershkowitz in 1999. He was **82 / 92** years old.

5 The oldest golf _____ in the world is in **the USA / Scotland**, where the sport started.

6 Yiannis Kouros holds the world record for the longest distance that anyone has run on an athletics _____ in 24 hours. In 1997, Yiannis ran **202 / 303** kilometres.

7 The fastest speed anyone has ever done on a skateboard wasn't on a skateboard _____, but on the road. The speed is **146 / 166** kilometres an hour.

1 Canada 2 150,000 3 42 4 82
5 Scotland 6 303 7 146

Need help? ➜ **Student's Book** page 171

GRAMMAR

Scan the QR code and watch the grammar animation.

1 Complete the sentences with the correct **gerunds**.

practising   jogging   ~~Climbing~~
diving   joining   spending

1 <u>Climbing</u> to the top of a really high mountain must be amazing!

2 I love _____ time with my cousins!

3 I fancy _____ a sports club, but I'm not sure which sport to choose.

4 If you want to become good at any sport, you need to keep _____ !

5 My uncle is mad about _____ – he runs five km every morning!

6 I've never tried _____ because I hate being under water.

Scan the QR code and watch the grammar animation.

2 Complete the sentences. Use **to** and the **infinitive**.

go   take   ~~do~~   swim   win   try

1 I think it is important <u>to</u> <u>do</u> exercise every day.

2 Maria learnt _____ _____ last year.

3 I can't wait _____ _____ part in my first judo competition.

4 Sasha wants _____ _____ salsa dancing.

5 We were losing 2–0, but we finally managed _____ _____ 3–2.

6 Last week, Sam persuaded me _____ _____ skateboarding with him.

3 Complete the text with the correct form of the verbs. Use the gerund or to and the infinitive.

Do something different!

(spend) <u>Spending</u> time on or near water is always fun, and most people enjoy **(try)** _____ new sports. So why not have a go at wakeboarding? Wakeboarding is like skateboarding, only on water. There are plenty of places where you can do it, so you can look online **(find)** <u>to find</u> a place near you. We advise people **(have)** _____ a few lessons so they can learn the basic skills. It's possible **(hire)** _____ a board at first, but it's worth **(buy)** _____ your own board as you get better, so you can practise **(do)** _____ more difficult moves. Wakeboarding can be dangerous, so it's important **(wear)** _____ a helmet. We also recommend **(wear)** _____ a wetsuit to keep you warm.

For more help, go to the Grammar reference:
→ **Student's Book** pages 220–221

→ 🔊 Go to page 110 to read the audioscript.

> ✅ **HELPFUL HINT FOR THIS TASK**
>
> - Look at the questions and highlight the key words.
> - Read the text and think about what words are missing.
> - Remember you can listen twice.

🔊 19 **You will hear a gym owner called Lee Norton talking about a spin class.**

For each question, write the correct answer in the gap.

Write one or two words or a number or a date or a time.

New Spin Class with VR (Virtual Reality)

Lee's gym introduced the VR spin class in **(1)** _____ .

Lee says the new VR spin class mixes exercise with **(2)** _____ .

When Lee tried the class himself, he found exercising less **(3)** _____ .

Lee says he most enjoyed the VR session involving cycling through the **(4)** _____ .

The best class for beginners is **(5)** _____ long.

Lee has plans for a VR class which offers the experience of **(6)** _____ .

For more help with Listening part 3:
→ **Student's Book Exam focus** page 73

READING

✔ HELPFUL HINT FOR THIS TASK

- Read the sentences and <u>underline</u> the key words.
- Draw lines between the paragraphs.
- Look at the **bold** words in the paragraphs.
- <u>Underline</u> words with the same meaning as the sentences.

1 **Read the article. Choose the best summary.**

A Joe Fuller still loves surfing in spite of a terrible experience.

B Joe Fuller encourages other surfers to learn from his experience and be more careful.

2 **Read the article again.**

Write ✓ (true) or ✗ (false).

1 Joe started surfing as soon as he moved to the coast. _____ ✗_

2 Joe says he loves surfing mainly because of how he feels when it goes well. _____

3 When Joe was carried out to sea, he wasn't sure what he should do. _____

4 Joe felt grateful when he was rescued, but also disappointed about losing his surfboard. _____

5 Joe had no fears about surfing again after his accident. _____

Mad about surfing

Joe Fuller can still clearly remember the first day he tried surfing. He was 14 years old. **He'd moved to the coast two years before** but wasn't very interested in sport at that time. Then some of his friends suggested going surfing one day in the summer holidays and he said yes. And that was it – he fell in love with the sport!

Joe says it's hard to describe what he thinks is so special about surfing. Obviously, it's wonderful to see the way the sea changes each day, so there are always new challenges to try. But according to Joe **the best thing is the amazing sense of freedom that you get when you're riding the perfect wave!**

But last year Joe had a terrifying experience. While he was surfing alone, the waves carried him out to sea, instead of bringing him back to the shore. Joe knew that it might be some time before rescuers found him, and he also knew the dangers of being in cold water for too long. **But he also knew he had no choice but to stay with his surfboard and wait.** Rescuers found him 16 hours later, nearly 20 kilometres away from the coast! He was cold and hungry, but still alive!

Joe says he can remember the mixture of feelings he had after he was rescued. He was exhausted, of course, and also quite **upset that there wasn't room in the rescue helicopter to bring his surfboard with him!** But most of all he **couldn't wait to thank all the people** who had worked so hard to find him and save his life.

And how did he feel about surfing again after his accident? **He admits that he was a little nervous about getting into the water again,** but once he rode his first wave the old excitement came back and he knew that stopping just wasn't an option!

(Circle) the correct words to complete the comments.

● ● ● ◁ ▷   🔍 🏠

sporty_jill Wow! What an amazing story. It really cheered me (**up**) / **out** to read about how brave Joe is! I think he should definitely stick **for** / (**at**) his surfing and enjoy it!

dunc_rose Reading about Joe made me want to **take** / **have** a go at surfing myself, though I'm sure I won't **learn** / **pick** it up very quickly!

seeseaemily I **got** / **made** into surfing a few years ago. I love it, but reading Joe's story has made me wonder if I should just chill **up** / **out** on the beach instead, where it's safe!

andy_surf Great story! Surfing is an amazing sport, once you **get** / **take** the hang of it. Yes, it can be dangerous, but it's also a great way to wind **down** / **off** when you're stressed.

SPEAKING

1 (Circle) the correct words.

1 I love rugby, (**so**) / **since** I watch a lot of rugby matches on TV.

2 I live near the sea, **because** / **which** is why it's easy for me to do water sports.

3 **So** / **Because** I'm quite a sociable person, I prefer team sports to individual sports.

4 I'm going to watch an athletics competition on Saturday, **since** / **so** I'm a big fan of athletics.

5 **As** / **So** I don't have much money, I can't afford to join a gym.

6 I love tennis **why** / **because** it's a really exciting sport.

2 Two people are talking about building a gym.

Complete the conversations.

~~agree~~   ~~What's~~

A: I think it would be good idea to build a gym in the town. <u>What's</u> your opinion?

B: I __agree__ with you. A gym would be a great idea.

should   right   that's

A: I think they _____ open a café at the gym. What do you think?

B: Yes, you're _____ . I think _____ a good idea.

sure   Really   How

A: _____ about an outdoor gym in the park?

B: _____ ? I'm not _____ that's the best idea.

WRITING

1 **Read the article about someone's favourite sport.**

Choose the best topic sentence for each paragraph.

A I first started climbing five years ago. _2_

B My favourite sport is climbing. __

C Climbing is great for people of any age. __

1 It's a popular sport all over the world. Some people climb high mountains with ropes to keep them safe. Other people prefer low climbing with no ropes. You can also practise the sport in some climbing gyms.

2 Some **friends invited me to go to the climbing gym** with them. I enjoyed it, so I decided to take it up. Since then, I've joined a climbing club and next year I'm going climbing in France with the club.

3 Young **children can start from the age of four or five**, and **people** can **continue** climbing when they're **quite old**. In fact, climbing is a very good way to stay fit and strong all through your life. Climbing is a great sport for everyone!

2 **Circle the correct connectors.**

1 Tennis is a fun sport to play. It's **too** / **also** a very exciting sport to watch.

2 I love singing **but** / **because** it always makes me feel cheerful.

3 I play **both** / **and** the guitar and the piano.

4 Last summer I went on some drama workshops **which** / **and** I enjoyed a lot.

5 Dancing is a great way to keep fit. It's really good fun **too** / **also**.

6 I love acting, **but** / **because** I always get really nervous before a show.

HOW WAS UNIT 13?

Gave it a go ☐

Getting there ☐

Aced it! ☐

14 ON TOP OF THE WORLD

VOCABULARY

1 Circle the correct adjectives.

1 I was really **disappointed** / **delighted** when my team lost the game.

2 We were all really **amused** / **shocked** when we saw how much damage the storm had done.

3 I always get really **satisfied** / **nervous** before exams.

4 I think we should do something to make Emma laugh. She looks really **miserable** / **impressed**!

5 It's important to talk to someone about your problems if you feel **depressed** / **jealous**.

2 Complete the text.

<del>impressed</del> cheerful guilty
jealous embarrassed

●●● ◄►   🔍 🏠

Do your feelings annoy you?

Mine do. For example, when a friend has done really well in a test and I haven't done so well. I want to feel pleased for him, and impressed with his achievement, but I can't help feeling just a little bit _____ of his success. Or when I see someone slip on the ice, I can't help laughing and then I feel really _____ because it's wrong to be mean! Or I might do something silly when other people are watching, so I feel really _____ and it spoils my _____ mood.

3 Circle the correct adjectives.

1 Matt's so rude sometimes. He shouts at people if he's angry, and he's also **cute** / **cruel** because he **treats** animals very badly.

2 Conor never thinks before he does things, so he does some really stupid things, but he's really kind and **fashionable** / **generous** – he **always** buys me nice presents!

3 Your little sister has got really lovely big eyes – she's so cute! I love her **long**, **clear** / **curly** hair, too!

4 Reece is really brave because he's never afraid to try new things, even if they're a bit dangerous. He's also very **patient** / **rude** with his annoying little sister.

Need help? → **Student's Book pages 179 and 181**

GRAMMAR

1 Complete the conditional sentences with the correct form of the verbs.

1 Dan **is** always in a bad mood if he **(lose)** _loses_ at computer games.

2 If Alice **wasn't** such a difficult person, more people **(like)** _____ her.

3 I **would be** delighted if I **(get)** _____ 90% in a maths test!

4 **I'll call** you if I **(manage)** _____ to get tickets for the show.

For more help, go to the Grammar reference:
→ **Student's Book** page 216

2 Complete the reported conversations with the correct verbs.

1	Adam: Where are you going?	Adam asked Lia where she (go) _was going_.
2	Lia: I'm going home.	Lia said that she (go) ____ ____ home.

3	Ella: Have you finished your project?	Ella asked Paul if he (finish) ____ ____ his project.
4	Paul: No, but I want to finish it by Friday.	Paul said no, but he said he (want) ____ to finish it by Friday.

5	Ana: Why did Emma leave the party?	Ana asked Amy why Emma (leave) ____ ____ the party.
6	Amy: I don't know.	Amy said that she (know) ____ ____ .

For more help, go to the Grammar reference:
→ **Student's Book** pages 211–213

3 Circle the correct modal verbs.

Teen Talk

I feel tired all the time and I **can't** / **couldn't** stay awake at school. I know I **ought** / **should** to get to bed earlier, but I keep getting messages from friends! **Lydia, 15**

Teen Talk's advice: You definitely **should** / **need** get more sleep. If you're too tired, your brain isn't **able** / **let** to work properly. Remember, you really **must** / **don't have to** answer messages immediately! You **can't** / **might** find it useful to leave your phone in the kitchen overnight.

My parents won't **let** / **make** me go out with my friends at the weekend. They say I **must** / **have** to help with our family restaurant. **Dean, 16**

Teen Talk's advice: Talk to them calmly and explain that you are almost an adult and they **shouldn't** / **need to** give you a bit more freedom.

4 Complete the relative clauses. Use *who, which, where* or *whose*.

1	It's important to thank people. **They** support you.	It's important to thank people _who_ support you.
2	Jen wants to show me the house. She grew up **there**.	Jen wants to show me the house ____ she grew up.
3	Tyler has offered to help with the food for the party. **His** dad is a chef.	Tyler, ____ dad is a chef, has offered to help with the food for the party.
4	The hotel was large. We stayed **in it**.	The hotel ____ we stayed in was quite large.
5	I passed all my exams. I was delighted about **it**.	I passed all my exams, ____ I was delighted about.
6	Stella always works hard at school. **She** wants to study law at university.	Stella, ____ wants to study law at university, always works hard at school.

For more help, go to the Grammar reference:
→ **Student's Book** pages 217–218

READING

✔ HELPFUL HINT FOR THIS TASK

● Read the sentence options 1–6 and <u>underline</u> the key words.

● Look at the **bold** words in the paragraphs 1–3.

● <u>Underline</u> words with the same meaning as the sentences.

1 Read the article. (Circle) the correct answers.

1 According to the writer,

  (A) we often experience more than one feeling in the same moment.

  B words are often more complicated than feelings.

2 In paragraph 2, the writer says that

  A there are too many different words for feelings.

  B sometimes words for feelings may be missing in our language.

3 You feel myötähäpeä

  A when you feel bad because you have done something foolish.

  B when you feel bad for another person.

4 Iktsuarpok is a feeling you get

  A when you are waiting for something bad to happen.

  B when you are looking forward to something.

5 Computers can already

  A help people to communicate through their minds.

  B see and understand people's feelings.

Feelings without words?

1 When someone asks you how you're feeling, do you sometimes find it hard to choose the right word to explain? That's not surprising, because feelings are complicated things and the words we use to describe them often seem too simple. For example, how do you feel when you fail an exam? Disappointed? Angry? Embarrassed? The chances are, **you feel all of these things at the same time** and there's no word that really describes what's going on in your head.

2 People have always found it difficult to put feelings into words, and sometimes what you're feeling may not even have a word in your language. **There are lots of different words for feelings in different languages**, like the Finnish word myötähäpeä, for example. This describes the feeling you get when **you see someone else doing something silly**, and you feel embarrassed for them! Or what about the Inuit word iktsuarpok, **which is that feeling of excitement you get when you're expecting someone** to arrive at your house, and you can't stop looking out of the window to see if they're coming. We recognise all these feelings, but of course **it's hard to explain them if our own language doesn't have a word for them.**

3 In the future, however, things might become easier. Scientists are working on computer systems that can 'read' people's thoughts. The computer 'watches' the electrical activity in someone's brain and then changes this into a digital message, which can be sent to another person. **Scientists in Spain have already managed to send the thought 'hello' from one brain to another in this way.** So, it's possible that in the future, when someone asks you how you're feeling, you might be able to turn a switch so that they can feel exactly what you're feeling, with no need to put it into words!

LISTENING PART 4

→ 🔊 Go to page 111 to read the audioscript.

> ✅ **HELPFUL HINT FOR THIS TASK**
>
> - Look at the questions and highlight the key words.
> - Draw lines between A, B and C.
> - Remember you can listen twice.

🔊 20 **For each question, choose the correct answer.**

You will hear an interview with a musician called Molly Ford talking about growing up with famous parents.

1 Molly first realised her parents were famous when

  A her family were followed by photographers.

  (B) she saw her parents' picture in a magazine.

  C fans stopped her parents in the street.

2 Although Molly enjoyed going on tour with her parents, she missed

  A her friends.

  B her daily routine.

  C her room at home.

3 How did Molly feel when she read articles about her parents?

  A angry because they said unpleasant things

  B pleased because she was mentioned in them

  C proud because so many people liked her parents

4 Molly remembers her parents often telling her that being famous

  A can have several advantages.

  B is never a permanent situation.

  C prevents you from having a normal life.

5 What does Molly say about her parents' famous friends?

  A They tell her lots of things about their lives.

  B They are just normal people to her.

  C They act differently in private and in public.

6 Molly thinks that if she has children in the future, she will

  A give up performing.

  B go travelling with them.

  C ask her parents to look after them.

For more help with Listening Part 4:

→ **Student's Book Exam Focus** page 99

PUSH YOURSELF B2

Complete with the compound nouns.

long-haired   highly respected
highly recommended   well-paid
blue-eyed   open-minded

1 There are nine _blue-eyed_ students in my class.

2 Joe's dad is a _____ artist.

3 She's now got a very _____ job.

4 My grandad's old, but he's still very _____.

5 I saw a photo of my dad when he was a _____ university student!

6 This is a _____ film, so we should go and see it.

SPEAKING

1 Complete the questions.

Can   How   Is   often   long   Why
Do   Which

1 _How_ do you usually get to school?

2 _Can_ you swim?

3 How _____ do you go shopping?

4 _____ you prefer to play sport or watch it?

5 How _____ have you known your best friend?

6 _____ it important to do exercise every week?

7 _____ do you enjoy going on holiday?

8 _____ is more fun, going to the cinema or watching a movie at home?

2 Circle the best answer to each question in exercise 1.

1 **(A)** I sometimes walk, or I get the bus if I'm late.

B I usually get to school at half past eight.

2 A No, I don't like swimming in the sea, but I like going to the swimming pool.

B Yes, I can. I'm quite a good swimmer.

3 A I usually go with my friends because they help me to choose new clothes.

B I don't go every week, but I go about once a month.

4 A I'm quite sporty, so I prefer to play sports myself.

B I like football and tennis, and I often watch them on TV.

5 A His name is James, and he's 15 years old, like me.

B I first met him when I was five, so I've known him for about 10 years.

6 A I think it's very important to do regular exercise, to keep fit and healthy.

B I go running every week because I think it's a good kind of exercise.

7 A I like it because when I'm on holiday I feel completely relaxed.

B I usually go to the beach and lie in the sun or swim in the sea.

8 A I often watch movies with my friends at home because we all like the same kinds of movies.

B I prefer to go to the cinema because films look more exciting on a big screen.

WRITING

1 Look at the student's plan for a profile of a friend.

Read sentences A–H and decide which two sentences should go in each paragraph (1–4).

Profile of Lily

1 her life and family   <u>D</u>   <u>H</u>

2 her appearance   —   —

3 her personality   —   —

4 things we do together   —   —

A She's very kind and friendly, and loves meeting new people.

B We sometimes watch films or play computer games together.

C She's quite tall, and she's got fair, curly hair.

D ~~Lily is my cousin and she lives in Amsterdam.~~

E Usually when we get together we just chat for hours!

F She loves clothes, so she always wears smart, fashionable clothes.

G She's also very intelligent and she wants to study medicine at university.

H ~~Her family moved there when she was three.~~

2 Read another student's profile of a friend. Circle the correct words.

Sarah is my best friend. She was born in France, **(but)** / **when** she moved to London with her family when she was seven years old. Now she goes to the same school as me, **(so)** / **because** I see her every day.

Although / **However** Sarah and I go to the same school, we are very different. Sarah has short, fair hair and wears very fashionable clothes. She's **too** / **also** very intelligent, and she wants to study business at university.

However / **So**, Sarah doesn't only think about herself and her career. She's very kind and generous, and she loves doing things to help other people.

We always have fun **because** / **when** we meet up. Sometimes we cook a meal together, as **well** / **or** we watch a film and then talk about it afterwards. I love talking to Sarah **because** / **so** she always has something interesting to say!

HOW WAS UNIT 14?

Gave it a go	⸢⸣
Getting there	⸢⸣
Aced it!	⸢⸣

AUDIOSCRIPT

STARTER

🌐 **Track 02**

Narrator: 1 – Maria

Maria: I love my job! I'm really interested in food, and I love cooking. I also like reading old cookery books and learning new ways to prepare food. But I don't want to work as a chef in a restaurant because you have to work at night – I like hanging out with my friends in the evenings! I usually have breakfast at eight o'clock and then start work. I start preparing a meal, then I get the video camera and start filming. A lot of people watch my shows online, which is great, and I'm starting to earn some money from them too. When I've got enough money, I want to visit different countries and learn different cooking skills, so I can use them in my vlogs.

Narrator: 2 – Sam

Sam: I enjoy lots of different sports, but tennis is my favourite. My parents are always saying to me, 'Why don't you become a sports teacher?' But I don't want to teach other people – I want to play myself! I'm winning quite a lot of games at the moment, so I really hope I can become a professional player. I'd love to see a photograph of myself in the newspaper one day, and read a report about one of my games! I have to watch what I eat, so I don't go to restaurants very often – pizzas aren't very good if you're serious about sport! I also listen to music a lot at home, and I sometimes go to concerts.

Narrator: 3 – Anika

Anika: My life is busy at the moment. I go to college three days a week, and I also work for a newspaper in my town. Not much happens in my town – there isn't much crime, so the police don't have much to do! But there are sometimes big sports events or music events. I enjoy writing reports about those. I think writing is my talent, so this is the right job for me. When I'm working, I always arrive at the office early, and they tell me which story to report. I talk to lots of different people for my job, which I enjoy. One day I might interview a doctor, then the next day I might talk to customers in a supermarket. Every day is different, which is great!

🌐 **Track 03**

1 I'm really interested in food.
2 I don't want to work as a chef in a restaurant.
3 I'm winning quite a lot of games at the moment.
4 I also listen to music a lot at home.
5 I also work for a newspaper in my town.
6 This is the right job for me.

UNIT 1

🌐 **Track 04**

Terry: Hi, and welcome to The Holiday Show. I'm Terry Maynard.

Lisa: And I'm Lisa Brighty.

Terry: Now, we're always looking for unusual holiday stories. Lisa, what have you found this week?

Lisa: Well, this is the story about the holiday company *Top Cruises*. As you know, a cruise is a luxury holiday on board a ship that travels around and visits different places. This company is now offering someone the chance to work as a professional tourist on their cruises!

Terry: So, you mean, they get paid to go on holiday?

Lisa: Exactly! The company runs seven different cruises during the summer, and they want someone to go on four of these cruises for them.

Terry: And what do they have to do? What's the 'job' part of it? Do they have to entertain the guests, or write a blog, something like that?

Lisa: No, they don't have to write anything. Believe it or not, all they have to do is post three photos a day on social media.

Terry: Really? That sounds like a really easy job! Can they be any kinds of photos?

Lisa: No. I thought it might be a bit boring, you know, just lots of photos of the ship to show how wonderful it is. But it has to be a mixture of scenery, people they meet and things they experience, either on the ship or when they visit places on the shore.

Terry: That doesn't sound like much work. Is there anything else?

Lisa: Yes. They have to make a short video to post on social media. This sounds a bit more difficult because the holiday company will choose a subject for them and they have to follow this.

Terry: That doesn't sound too bad. And what do they receive in return?

Lisa: They get all their travel expenses, of course, and all their food, and also spending money of about £1,000 a week, so they can buy things to remind them of their trip.

Terry: Wow! So, why is the company doing this?

Lisa: Well, it certainly isn't because their cruise ships are empty! They know that most people who want to go on a cruise look online for ideas. So they want to get lots of amazing photos of their cruises onto the internet, so that when people start searching, they'll find them and decide to book their own trip.

Terry: And how will they choose the right person for the job? Does it have to be someone who knows a lot about travel?

Lisa: No, they want someone who can take good photos and show that they've had an amazing time. So, if you want to apply, you don't send a letter – just email some examples of your own holiday posts. And you never know, you might just get this dream job. I think I might apply myself!

UNIT 2
🔊 **Track 05**

Narrator: For each question, choose the correct answer.

1 – You will hear two friends talking about a film they have just seen.

Man: So, did you enjoy that?

Woman: It was certainly different to the movies we normally go to. I enjoyed the special effects, but they were so noisy in places, it spoiled my enjoyment. I missed a lot of what the characters were saying to each other, so I didn't know what was going on. It was such a shame. I'm sure we've seen the leading actor in something else.

Man: Yeah, she was in that romantic comedy last month. You know, the one that felt like it went on for hours and hours.

Woman: Oh yes, I remember. That wasn't great either.

Narrator: Now listen again.

Narrator: 2 – You will hear a brother and sister talking about booking concert tickets.

Woman: I guess we need to book seats for the concert soon. Otherwise they'll be sold out.

Man: Well, here's the seating plan on the website. Lots of seats on the left- or right-hand sides of the hall.

Woman: Hardly surprising, you can't see properly unless you get seats in the centre. Look, there's a couple free in the middle of the fourth row. How fantastic!

Man: But look at the price! Let's see what's available in the balcony.

Woman: Mm, quite a few, but they're not much cheaper.

Man: OK. Then I think it's worth paying a bit more.

Woman: Absolutely.

Narrator: Now listen again.

Narrator: 3 – You will hear a woman telling a friend about a TV programme.

Woman: Tim, did you watch TV last night? There was a fantastic programme on.

Man: No, I was out.

Woman: Shame. It was filmed on a Scottish island – the one where they made your favourite police detective dramas – I can't remember the name of the programme – and it was about a group of people there and how they're trying to live without electricity, cars, and so on, and growing all their own food. And of course, the scenery was really dramatic.

Man: Sounds interesting. I'll try and watch it next week.

Woman: It was just a single show, but it's probably available online.

Narrator: Now listen again.

Narrator: 4 – You will hear two people talking about online newspapers.

Man: What are you reading?

Woman: An article on my favourite newspaper website. It's really good for news about sport.

Man: Yes, I always get my news online now. I mean, for people who haven't got much time or only want the basic facts, it's better to catch the news headlines on the television. I've noticed, though, that all news programmes and newspapers cover the same issues, but if you want full explanations and answers to the real questions, you have to *read* the news rather than listen to it.

Woman: Yes, that's probably true.

Narrator: Now listen again.

Narrator: 5 – You will hear a man telling a friend about a play called *The Visit*.

Man: I finally went to a performance of *The Visit* at the theatre last night. I was so looking forward to it. Eddy Smith is my favourite director and I've waited ages to go to another of his productions.

Woman: And what was it like?

Man: Different to his usual work, but it made me think a lot. And at least I can now join in conversations when people are discussing it.

Woman: Well, please don't tell me how it finishes because I'm going to see it next week.

Man: I won't say a word.

Narrator: Now listen again.

Narrator: 6 – You will hear two friends talking about a summer music festival.

Woman: I've got my ticket for this year's Fun in the Sun festival.

Man: You go every year, don't you?

Woman: Yeah, it's my favourite event of the summer. Since it started getting more popular, it costs loads more to get in. But then I don't have to pay to get there as it's only down the road from my parents' house. People who come from further away often get stuck in traffic for ages.

Man: Perhaps I'll get tickets this year too.

Woman: Great. We can arrange to meet somewhere there. Otherwise we'll never see each other among the hundreds of people.

Narrator: Now listen again.

Narrator: That is the end of Part 2.

UNIT 3
🕑 Track 06

Presenter: Hi and welcome to The Food Show. Today I'm talking to Elsa Brooks, a food journalist. Nice to have you here.

Elsa: It's great to be here.

Presenter: And you're going to tell us about a very different restaurant in New York. What's different about this restaurant, Elsa?

Elsa: Well, it's a normal restaurant in some ways – you order food from a waiter and pay your bill at the end. But the people who cook the food aren't professional chefs, so they have no training. They are all grandmothers – ordinary women who are used to cooking everyday food for their families, so the kind of food you eat there is the kind of delicious traditional food your own grandmother might cook for you.

🕑 Track 07

Presenter: So how did you first learn about this restaurant, Elsa?

Elsa: Well, as you know I read restaurant reviews all the time, and I'm always looking for new restaurants to try, but I didn't know about this one until a friend mentioned it to me, and I thought: I have to go there! You don't see many advertisements for it, so I'm really glad I found out about it.

Presenter: Now, the owner is called Mr Scaravella, I believe. Why did he want to start a restaurant with grandmothers for cooks?

Elsa: Well, clearly there are a lot of great restaurants in New York, and people eat out all the time and spend a lot of money on eating out. But actually Mr Scaravella started this restaurant because his own grandmother had died, and he had wonderful memories of eating her home-cooked food.

Presenter: So, what's the menu like?

Elsa: Well, Mr Scaravella is Italian, and half the menu is Italian food, cooked by Italian grandmothers – that doesn't change. Then the other half of the menu is cooked by a different grandmother every night, and they come from all over the world, and cook their own traditional dishes from their countries. And the people who go there to eat love *all* these different dishes!

Presenter: So, tell us about the different women who cook at the restaurant.

Elsa: Well, there's always a main cook for the night, and then a helper, usually someone from a different country. And the great thing is that because the food they cook is all so different, they don't compete with each other to try to be the best. They really enjoy trying the dishes the other women cook, and they learn little tips from each other, about new things they can try.

Presenter: And they also have cooking classes there, don't they?

Elsa: Yes. The classes are run by the grandmothers who cook there, and they're a chance for them to share their skills and their recipes. The classes are all female. They aren't too expensive, but they are very popular, so you need to book well in advance.

Presenter: And finally, how was your experience of eating in the restaurant?

Elsa: Oh, it was amazing! There was a great atmosphere, and everyone was really friendly – the waiters, especially. I managed to talk to some of the other guests too, which was nice. But the food was the best bit. It was amazing – really good, home-cooked dishes. The cook was Japanese the evening I was there, and I'll definitely go back and hopefully try a dish from a different country!

UNIT 4
🔊 **Track 08**

Narrator: For each question, choose the correct answer.

1 – Where will the woman go camping this summer?

Man: Are you camping again this summer?

Woman: Yes, but we're trying somewhere new. We've camped at the same place up in the mountains for the last three years, and it's been great going for walks in the forest. But that site's closed now, so we're staying on a farm.

Man: That sounds really peaceful.

Woman: Oh, I imagine the animals will wake us up really early. It was either camp in the field, or by the river, and I thought the sound of water would keep me awake all night.

Narrator: Now listen again.

Narrator: 2 – What's the view from the apartment block?

Man: Hi, Pete. I've just arrived at my holiday apartment. It's right in the city centre, in what must be the tallest building around. There are windows on two sides and they're huge. Across the square I can see an enormous statue of someone – I'm not sure who, but I'll go down and look later. I want to find out about taxis too because there's a famous bridge somewhere in this part of town that I want to go across. I'll send you some photos.

Narrator: Now listen again.

Narrator: 3 – Which activity did the woman help with?

Man: How was your weekend?

Woman: Great, but I'm exhausted now. I've become a volunteer for a charity that looks after the countryside. You know, doing things like cutting down plants that are growing in the wrong place and making it difficult for walkers to use the paths. I spent all weekend clearing rubbish out of streams and I'm going back next weekend as they need volunteers to rebuild some of the old field walls.

Narrator: Now listen again.

Narrator: 4 – Where will the friends meet before going to the theatre?

Woman: Will you have enough time to meet and go for a pizza before we go to the theatre tomorrow evening?

Man: Probably not. My last lecture doesn't finish till six-fifteen.

Woman: Well, l if you're coming straight from the university, I'll wait for you by the art gallery.

Man: OK, I should be there around 7.

Woman: I think I'll go shopping before I meet you. And I can get a takeaway pizza in the shopping centre.

Man: OK. See you at 7 then.

Narrator: Now listen again.

Narrator: 5 – Where is the problem in the apartment building?

Woman: So this is your apartment building. The entrance is very modern, and the automatic doors make it look really smart.

Man: Yes, I don't know how I'd get in if they stopped working. I think there's probably someone to call if I have any problems. Actually, I need to do that already because when you come out of the lift, it's really dark in the hall outside my flat. The light bulb needs changing.

Woman: Well, do you want to phone someone before we go in?

Man: I will, if you don't mind waiting.

Narrator: Now listen again.

Narrator: 6 – What did the woman do in the park?

Woman: Hi, Natalie. I'm phoning because I was in the park this morning – I'd gone there to do some reading but the seats by the fountain were gone because they were doing some repairs to it. Anyway, I'd just finished taking pictures of these beautiful flowers and as I stood up, a jogger ran past me. You won't believe it, but I've just realised that it was Daniel from school. He must be back from Australia. Do you still have his number?

Narrator: Now listen again.

Narrator: 7 – Where in the city will they eat tonight?

Man: Do you mind where we go for a meal this evening?

Woman: I'd rather not go to a fast food place. I hate the long queues there and anyway I'd prefer something a bit healthier than burgers and fries. There's a food truck by the river that sells sushi. It shouldn't be too busy, and it's certainly cheaper than eating in a restaurant.

Man: Sounds good to me. I'm not exactly dressed for anywhere really smart.

Woman: Me neither. And also it's a lovely place to go for a walk afterwards.

Narrator: Now listen again.

Narrator: That is the end of Part 1.

UNIT 5
🎧 **Track 09**

Elly: Hi, I'm Elly Barlow, and today we're talking about fitness. Now, I'm not as fit as I should be, and I hate the gym! But there are lots of apps that promise to get you fit in just a few minutes each day. Is that possible? With me is Jake Milburn, a personal trainer. He's tried four apps for us. What did you find, Jake?

Jake: Well, the first one I chose is 'Ten-minute Yoga'. Each day it gives you a new workout with ten different exercises, which take one minute each. The idea is to make your body stronger and able to move more easily. You have to hold each position for as long as possible, for a minute if you can. One problem is that there's no voice, so you have to read the instructions. That's difficult while you're doing the exercises.

Elly: Will it get me fit?

Jake: No, you need to work harder than this to get fit.

Elly: OK. What's next?

Jake: 'Daily Fit Club' has 12-minute workouts to make your heart and muscles stronger. The exercises are quite difficult, and they'll definitely make your heart work. One problem is that the exercises have strange names like 'tuck jumps' and 'air jacks'. The instructor just calls out these names, so you need to learn all the names before you try the workouts. Also, you have to be quite fit before you start, so it isn't really suitable for beginners.

Elly: No good for me, then.

Jake: Probably not. The next one is 'Burn the Fat'. This has 10-minute workouts that aim to burn body fat and make you thinner and fitter. The workouts aren't easy, and they feel much longer than 10 minutes. I'm pretty fit, and I got hot and out of breath! The exercises are good, but they're not very interesting and you repeat them lots of times. I think most people would lose interest and give up on this one!

Elly: Definitely no good for me, then. What about the last one?

Jake: This was 'Superfit in Ten'. I loved this. It's for beginners, and it uses videos to show you what to do, so it's clear and easy to follow. The exercises start easy and get harder as you do more workouts. The workouts are fun, they'll definitely get your heart beating fast, and your muscles will get stronger.

Elly: It sounds like a good one for me.

Jake: Yeah, it's a great app for you, and will definitely get you fitter, but only if you use it every day!

Elly: Thanks, Jake.

UNIT 6
🔊 **Track 10**

Narrator: For each question, write the correct answer in the gap. Write one or two words or a number or a date or a time.

You have twenty seconds to look at Part 3.

You will hear a journalist called Steffi talking about a week she spent without using social media.

Steffi: I'm Steffi and I'd like to tell you about something I did recently – I gave up social media for a whole week.

When I was at school, I was too busy with activities at home to use social media. I saw my friends every day anyway. Then, when I went to university, I wanted to keep in contact with people back home, so that's when I first went on social media.

Mostly I used social media for reading friends' messages. Instead of writing long replies, I put selfies on my social media page. People could see where I was and how much fun I was having.

When I started working, I noticed I was using social media loads more. It was probably only 10 minutes at a time. But in a day, it was more than two hours. I decided to write an article about social media. I interviewed people, and some said they used social media for three hours a day.

Anyway, last week I stopped going on social media completely. I knew I needed something else to read, and I'm not a big fan of reading magazines, so I chose a novel. And I really enjoyed it.

At the beginning of the week, I expected to feel worried about not knowing what friends were doing. But I had more time to call people, and I met some friends after work, which was lovely. At the end of seven days, I definitely wasn't as stressed, even though it was really busy at work.

So, will I change my social media habits? Well, I've deleted almost all social media apps from my phone. I'm going to check the news app, but only in the evening for no more than twenty minutes. And I definitely plan to see friends more.

Narrator: Now listen again.

Narrator: That is the end of Part 3.

UNIT 7
🎧 **Track 11**

Kiera: Hi. Welcome to The World of Clothes. I'm Kiera Samson, and this is my weekly podcast on everything to do with clothes and fashion. And usually I'm talking about things like where to find clothes that look good, or clothes that are good value and not too expensive to buy. But this week I want to talk about something a bit different – ethical clothes – that means, clothes that are made in a good way – a way that doesn't harm the planet, so they don't cause pollution, and they treat people well too, by paying fair wages and giving people good working conditions.

🎧 **Track 12**

Kiera: So, I've been looking at ethical clothes online, and there are some great ideas out there. For example, there's a really stylish pair of blue trainers here. What's special about them? Well, we all know that there's a huge amount of waste plastic in the ocean, and it's damaging marine animals. So now one company is using this plastic waste to make trainers. You can get them in different colours and I must say they look pretty trendy. The company that makes them is making a real effort to help the environment. For example, last year they completely stopped using plastic bags in their shops – they only use paper ones now, and that's got to be a good thing!

Now, if trainers aren't your thing, maybe food is. Food and clothes, you're asking – what's that about? Well, a company in Sweden that makes outdoor clothes is trying to deal with the problem of all the clothes we throw away. As you know, a lot of the rubbish we throw away is buried in the ground, and most modern clothes stay there for hundreds of years. But this company's clothes are all made from completely natural materials, so when they go into the ground as rubbish, they break down, and you can even grow vegetables in the waste they produce. Cool, eh? Their clothes are expensive, of course, and a lot of people can't afford to buy them, but another good thing about them is that they allow you to *rent* them cheaply, and you can give them back when you've finished using them!

Another website that I found is called GoodClothes.com, and this sells all kinds of clothes that are made in an ethical way. There are different signs next to the clothes that tell you what's good about each item. For example, a lot of their clothes are made without any animal products, so they're perfect if you're a vegetarian, or you care about animals. Other signs show that the people who make the clothes get a fair wage for their work, or the clothes are made with local materials. There are some really cool T-shirts on there, and I'd love to buy one, but I'm afraid they're just too expensive for me.

So, that's it for this week. I hope I've given you some things to think about. Bye for now, and happy shopping!

UNIT 8

🔊 **Track 13**

Narrator: For each question, choose the correct answer.

You have 45 seconds to look at the questions for Part 4.

Presenter: I'm talking to Rob Tucker, a wildlife expert who's studied camels in Australia. Rob, how did you get interested in camels?

Rob: I've been interested in all animals that were introduced into Australia by Europeans – camels, buffaloes, rabbits, horses and sheep of course – for quite a long time. When I was a student, a movie came out about a woman called Robyn Davidson who crossed an Australian desert with four camels. I actually missed it but someone gave me a book she'd written about her adventure – I really enjoyed it and it made me want to learn more about these amazing creatures.

Presenter: When did camels arrive in Australia?

Rob: One was brought here in 1840. Then, in the 1860s, many more arrived on ships. To start with, they came with camel farmers who knew how to handle and train them. Camel farms were set up and soon there were thousands of camels – the perfect animal to help explorers discover Australia. Camels born on the farms worked harder and carried more than the original camels. I should mention those camels were mostly from India. It's easy to forget camels aren't just from Arabian countries.

Presenter: Why were camels so useful? I know they don't need water every day.

Rob: Well, there's water even in the desert. For me, camels had the advantages of horses – they could carry people and equipment over rough countryside – but they had the added benefit of keeping going all day, stopping to rest only at night.

Presenter: Not all Australians today like camels, do they?

Rob: No. Most camels today are wild. There's hundreds of thousands of them – and that's a problem for sheep and cow farmers. Some parts of Australia haven't had rain for several years. Camels go onto farms and dig holes to get to pipes carrying water to farmhouses and to where sheep and cows go to drink. So farmers are always having to do repairs.

Presenter: Camels are also a tourist attraction, aren't they?

Rob: Yeah … if you haven't tried a camel ride, you should. It's amazing to ride into the desert and camp under the stars for two nights, returning only at the end of the third day. Obviously, if visitors don't have much time, they go for a day, or even take half-day trips, but I don't think that's enough.

Presenter: How easy is it to see camels in the wild?

Rob: Surprisingly difficult, especially if you're driving along the road, even though their numbers are still growing. The thing is, they're more or less the same brown as the countryside. This makes them very easy to miss, especially if they're not moving.

Presenter: Of course …

Narrator: Now listen again.

Narrator: That is the end of Part 4.

UNIT 9

⊘ **Track 14**

Presenter: Welcome to the show. Today we're talking about learning as an adult, and with me is Stella Bradshaw. Her book, *Never too late to learn*, was published last month. Stella, why did you write the book?

Stella: Well, I first went to university when I was 26. I wasn't a 'good student' at school, and for me it was a great achievement to finally get my degree. It made me realise that learning isn't just for school. It's something you can do all your life. I wanted to encourage other people to keep learning!

Presenter: Is it difficult to study as an adult?

Stella: No. Colleges and universities welcome older students. Last year a degree was awarded to Mavis Bowman, who's 86! She left school at 15, mainly because her parents needed her to work to help pay the bills. She was never really interested in learning, and it was only when her grandson asked her for help with a project that she realised what a pleasure learning was, and decided to get a degree.

Presenter: That's amazing! Is it harder to learn when you're older?

Stella: It can be slightly more difficult to remember things, like facts, but this doesn't mean that older people learn more slowly. In general they work harder than younger people, so they learn just as fast – remember, they're learning because they want to, not because they have to.

Presenter: Now, the book also deals with other kinds of learning, like learning a language, art, music, or sport. Why do you think it's so important to keep learning?

Stella: Learning something new helps you feel more confident – can you remember that amazing feeling you had as a child when you managed to do something new for the first time? But most of all, it stops life from getting boring!

Presenter: You interviewed a lot of people for the book, and there are some great stories. What's your favourite?

Stella: I think that's Kevin Jones, who learned to ride a bike at the age of 28. He describes how difficult it was and what the experience taught him, like it's OK to admit you can't do something, and you shouldn't judge other people, and, most importantly, sometimes there are no quick solutions and you have to keep trying if you want to succeed.

Presenter: Finally, what's your advice for our listeners?

Stella: Never think that something is too difficult for you. If you couldn't do it in the past, it doesn't mean you can't do it now. So if you want to play a musical instrument or take up a sport, learn a language, or get a degree: just do it!

UNIT 10

⬢ Track 15

Narrator: 1.

Woman: I ride my bike everywhere, and I think these new cycle paths are great. It's dangerous to ride on the main roads because most car drivers don't pay attention to bikes. Having proper cycle paths is much better. I like the fact that there are lights, too, which means you can use them even when it's dark, and you know you aren't in any danger.

Narrator: 2.

Man: I've tried using the new cycle paths, because it would be great for me if I could get to work by bike every day. They're OK, and I guess I'll get used to them. But I think they need to put some signs up to help people see which way to go, especially through the park. It isn't always clear at the moment.

Narrator: 3.

Woman: Well, it's good to see that the city is trying to do more to encourage people to use their bikes. But I really don't think they've done very well with these. They're too narrow, which means they're difficult to use when there are a lot of bikes, and they don't go to places where anyone wants to go. To be honest, I think they're a complete waste of time!

Narrator: 4.

Man: I've used them quite a lot. There are plenty of them, and there's one that goes very close to the place where I work. It's great to be able to avoid the main roads, but in a way, I think they've been too successful. There are so many bikes on them in the mornings that it almost feels as if you're riding on a busy road!

⬢ Track 16

Narrator: For each question, choose the correct answer.

1 – You will hear two friends talking about a new airport.

Man: Wow, this is an amazing airport! How long has it been open?

Woman: Only about two or three months. I love the design of the building, although I thought we were going to get lost when we were driving in.

Man: Yes, the information was quite confusing. But they've clearly put a lot of thought into collecting rubbish – with separate bins for plastic, paper, food, and so on.

Woman: And you don't have to look around to find them. It's just a shame the airport's on the opposite side of the city to where we live.

Man: At least we don't hear any noise.

Narrator: Now listen again.

Narrator: 2 – You will hear a woman telling her brother about her new electric bicycle.

Woman: I rode my new electric bike to college today.

Man: And?

Woman: Well, people who don't know me don't know that I have to cycle up those really steep hills near our house. And it's really flat around college. So I felt a bit uncomfortable – I mean it makes me look lazy. I'm sure people were looking at me as I parked it with the other bikes.

Man: I wouldn't worry about that.

Woman: I can't help it. Still, the bike's great quality. If I look after it, I should be able keep it for years.

Narrator: Now listen again.

Narrator: 3 – You will hear two colleagues talking about travelling to work.

Woman: There must be something happening in town today. Do you know, it took me 15 minutes to find a parking space this morning! Do you still catch the train to work?

Man: Yes. I'd never go back to driving. Sitting in traffic at the end of the day used to make me so cross.

Woman: I guess it must be useful to be able to send emails and read reports on the train before you even get to work.

Man: I only read for pleasure in the mornings.

Narrator: Now listen again.

Narrator: 4 – You will hear two friends talking about getting to the airport.

Man: Julia, about going to the airport next week … Last time we arranged to meet by the entrance it took us ages to find each other.

Woman: Yes, there was a huge tour group there. So why don't I come to your house?

Man: I can't make you do that. It would mean a very long journey for you. I was going to say, maybe we should look at the airport plan and find a better place to meet – like by the bus station, or the pick-up point.

Woman: Yes. Let's check online now.

Narrator: Now listen again.

Narrator: 5 – You will hear two neighbours talking about traffic in the town.

Woman: I'm so glad the roadworks are finished now. The traffic jams were awful.

Man: Hmm, there was someone on the radio saying wider roads simply encourage more traffic. The issue for me is that local people will get used to the new one-way system, but if you don't know the town, it's so easy to get lost now.

Woman: And you can't just turn around.

Man: Well, it's too late to change it now.

Woman: Perhaps they should build a huge car park on the edge of town.

Man: They talked about doing that once before, but the shop owners were against it.

Narrator: Now listen again.

Narrator: 6 – You will hear two friends talking about recycling.

Woman: Tom, is that a new water bottle?

Man: Yes, it's made of metal. It means I don't have to buy plastic bottles of water when I'm out.

Woman: I might get one of those. I've already got a cup made of bamboo, for when I'm out and want to get a coffee. Plastic's such a big problem, isn't it? I mean, some things I buy at the shop only come in bottles made of plastic. And I've almost given up buying things in jars because glass isn't environmentally friendly to produce.

Man: Oh, I know. It's impossible to know what to do sometimes.

Narrator: Now listen again.

Narrator: That is the end of Part 2.

UNIT 11

⊘ Track 17

Presenter: Welcome to the show. Living in London isn't easy, but with me today are three young people who are happy with how they've chosen to live in the capital. First, Ewan, a designer. Where do you live?

Ewan: I live in an empty office block. People often think it's against the law, but I rent through an agency. The owners prefer to have people living there, to keep the building safe until a business moves in. The advantage is that the rent is really cheap, and I don't have to travel far to work. The disadvantage is there's only one office toilet for 12 people on my floor, and the only shower is one we've set up ourselves. Also, I might have to move out at any time if a business wants to move in. But it's worth it because I can save money to get my own place.

Presenter: That's really interesting. Now Daisy, a nurse, has found a different way to live. Tell us where you live, Daisy.

Daisy: I live with an 89-year-old lady, Julie, in her house. Lots of elderly people live alone in London, and they're often lonely. Sharing the house with a young person is a good solution – cheap rent in return for friendship. So, from Monday to Friday, I cook with Julie in the evenings, or we go out for a meal. Actually, she's great fun, and she's given me lots of useful advice about all kinds of things. The disadvantages? It was difficult at first because I wasn't used to living with someone older, but it's fine now. And I've saved lots of money! I'm moving out soon, into my own flat, but Julie and I have become friends, so I'll still see her.

Presenter: What a lovely story. And finally, Andy, a musician. Tell us about your home.

Andy: I live on a boat on the river. I bought it last year, and I love it! The main advantages are that it's cheap and it's my own, so I can decorate it or do whatever I want with it. The disadvantages are that I have to look after it and do repairs, and emptying the toilet every week isn't much fun! It wouldn't suit someone who likes to live somewhere comfortable! The other problem is that I have to move around. You're only allowed to stay in one place for 14 days, then you have to move. But, on the positive side, I've made lots of friends with other young people who are doing the same thing as me – that's really nice.

UNIT 12

⊘ Track 18

Narrator: For each question, choose the correct answer.

1 – What is the woman's job now?

Woman: I'm really interested in buildings and their history. For a few years, I taught on a local history course at the university in my city. I really enjoyed sharing my knowledge with students but I didn't enjoy being indoors every day. Now I share what I know with visitors to the city by leading walking tours around all the important buildings – old and new – in the city centre.

Narrator: Now listen again.

Narrator: 2 – Which benefit does the man's company offer staff?

Woman: Are you glad you moved to a new company?

Man: Absolutely. It's a great firm to work for. There's a free car park for staff, which has made my journey to work a lot easier. And another thing they provide is free health checks twice a year. I've got my first one next month, so I've decided to join a gym – I don't want to be told I'm unfit.

Woman: What a good idea.

Narrator: Now listen again.

Narrator: 3 – Who works in the sales department?

Woman: I work in the sales department of a small company that makes equipment for hospitals. My manager's called Anna, and I get on really well with her. There used to be two men as well, but one of them left. That's made things really busy recently, but we're supposed to be getting another member of staff soon. My friend Sally has applied for the job but she hasn't heard yet if she's got an interview.

Narrator: Now listen again.

Narrator: 4 – Where does the man work?

Woman: Are you still working at the art gallery?

Man: No, that was just a part-time job while I was looking for something more permanent. There's a shopping centre that's opening next week behind the art gallery, and they've hired me to be head of security.

Woman: That's great. When do you start?

Man: Actually, I already have. It's great – it's the same journey time as the gallery, and when the centre opens, I'll be able to have lunch in a different restaurant every day.

Woman: Perhaps we could meet for lunch one day.

Man: Sure.

Narrator: Now listen again.

Narrator: 5 – What does the woman like best about her job?

Man: How are you getting on at work?

Woman: Fine. I've been promoted. I'm now personal assistant to the accountant. I don't have my own office but that's OK because the people I share an office with are quite nice. And the company recently installed this *amazing* new accounts software. It makes going to work every day a pleasure.

Man: The views must be great – I mean, isn't your office on the top floor?

Woman: Yes, you can see right across the city. To be honest, I rarely have time for looking out the window.

Narrator: Now listen again.

Narrator: 6 – What was the man's career ambition when he was a child?

Man: When I was a kid, I dreamed of running away from school and getting a boat and sailing round the world. I also used to race round the garden being a train driver, telling everyone that's what I was going to be when I grew up. When I was eight, I remember my parents taking me on a helicopter ride – I loved the speed and the sense of feeling free. I still get that feeling in my job as a pilot, especially when I look out of the plane at the ground below.

Narrator: Now listen again.

Narrator: 7 – Who is the woman's sister?

Man: What's your sister doing now she's left college? She wanted to work in television, didn't she?

Woman: Oh, she's opened her own café!

Man: I bet the food's delicious. She was always a great cook.

Woman: Well actually she's got a couple of people who run the kitchen. It means she has time to work out front, chatting to customers about what they like.

Man: I can see her being brilliant at that. She's confident and she has good people skills.

Narrator: Now listen again.

Narrator: That is the end of Part 1.

UNIT 13
🔊 **Track 19**

Narrator: For each question, write the correct answer in the gap. Write one or two words or a number or a date or a time. You have twenty seconds to look at Part 3.

Narrator: You will hear a gym owner called Lee Norton talking about a spin class.

Lee: I'm Lee Norton from Norton's Gym. I'd like to tell you about a class we're offering – a spin class with virtual reality. I hope you'll decide to join.

For those of you who haven't heard of spinning, it's indoor cycling on a machine, and it gives you a great workout. We've offered ordinary spin classes since January, when the gym opened. I did a spin class with virtual reality when I visited New York in May – I loved it and had to have it in my gym. Finally, in August, we were ready to open the class.

If you haven't done spin with virtual reality, it's like a spin class but in the dark, and you watch a huge screen as you cycle. I describe it as a way to enjoy fitness *and* cinema – it's not often you can do those two things together.

Spin with virtual reality is a fantastic workout. People who've tried it said it wasn't as boring as regular exercise because they had something else to think about. I personally thought it made the whole thing less painful, and the time went more quickly than in a traditional class.

So what do you watch while you're doing the spin class? We have several 'programmes' and I've tried them all. We change these regularly to keep it interesting. One week there's a ride through the countryside, or the city – my personal favourite – or on a race track.

If you're new to spin classes, I'd suggest the level one class, which lasts thirty-five minutes. It's best to arrive fifteen minutes early for the first session, so you can meet the instructor. You'll soon be ready to manage the next level, which is forty-five minutes long.

Customers tell me how much they like the virtual reality classes, so I'm intending to offer a wider choice of virtual reality fitness activities than just cycling, starting with running. And if that's popular, we might consider rowing classes.

Narrator: Now listen again.

Narrator: That is the end of Part 3.

UNIT 14

🔊 **Track 20**

Narrator: For each question, choose the correct answer.

You have 45 seconds to look at the questions for Part 4.

Narrator: You will hear an interview with a musician called Molly Ford, talking about growing up with famous parents.

Presenter: My guest today is singer-songwriter Molly Ford. Welcome, Molly.

Molly: Thank you.

Presenter: Your parents are successful musicians too. When you were growing up, at what point did you realise they were famous?

Molly: All through my childhood, people came up to chat to them in the street. I just thought everyone was being friendly. Once, at a friend's house, there was a music magazine on the table. Mum and Dad were on the cover. I thought 'wow, they must be real stars'. I don't remember photographers following them. Maybe I didn't notice.

Presenter: What was it like touring with your parents?

Molly: An adventure. No two days were the same, you never felt stuck in a routine. I had mates, because the other musicians in the band took their families too. Sometimes staying in hotels was annoying. I wanted to sleep in my own bed and have my things around me. I hated leaving my toys behind when I was little.

Presenter: Did you ever read stuff about your parents when you were growing up?

Molly: My parents gave lots of interviews and were always open. I don't remember them ever getting cross because of lies about them in the newspapers. They were very proud of me, and still are – and it was kind of lovely to see things they'd said about me.

Presenter: Have your parents given you advice about being famous?

Molly: When I was a teenager, I got embarrassed if classmates kept asking me questions about them. Mum and Dad encouraged me to see the positive sides of being famous – the money, the chances to meet celebrities, and so on. Apart from that, we didn't talk about it. We were a happy family. Living out of suitcases was a temporary thing, but it was normal to us.

Presenter: I imagine your parents had famous friends.

Molly: Yes – I still see them now. They're interested in my career, and are great at listening to me if I have problems. It makes me laugh when I see them doing ordinary things, like washing up – I can't help thinking 'you're a worldwide superstar'. When I watch them on TV, I notice they don't behave the same as at home – they're more careful in what they say and do.

Presenter: Interesting. If you have children one day, will you take them on tour?

Molly: I don't know. I love working in the music industry, but travelling's tiring. Most probably I'd move into music producing or write songs for other people. I'd like to think my parents could be babysitters, but they'll probably still be touring!

Presenter: And what…

Narrator: Now listen again.

Narrator: That is the end of Part 4.

ACKNOWLEDGEMENTS

The authors and publishers would like to thank: Phil Dexter, Inclusive Education Consultant, and Orsolya Misik-Szatzker, teacher specialising in language learning for dyslexic students, for their insights and expertise during the development process.

Lucy Passmore and Jishan Uddin for their contribution to the grammar animations.

The authors and publishers acknowledge the following sources of copyright material and are grateful for the permissions granted. While every effort has been made, it has not always been possible to identify the sources of all the material used, or to trace all copyright holders. If any omissions are brought to our notice, we will be happy to include the appropriate acknowledgements on reprinting and in the next update to the digital edition, as applicable.

Key: ST = Starter, U = Unit

Text
U2: Guardian News and Media Limited for the text from 'How Marvel's superheroes found the magic to make us all true believers' by Jeffrey A Brown, *The Guardian*, 31/08/2013. Copyright Guardian News & Media Ltd 2013.

Photography
The following images are sourced from Getty Images.

UST: Klaus Vedfelt/DigitalVision; Jetta Productions Inc./DigitalVision; Robin Skjoldborg/Cultura; Nikada/E+; monkeybusinessimages/iStock/Getty Images Plus; andresr/E+; **U1:** Holger Leue/Lonely Planet Images; Leland Bobbe/Stockbyte; Westend61; Eva-Katalin/E+; Daniel Schoenen/Look; Art Wager/E+; **U3:** guruxoox/iStock/Getty Images Plus; LauriPatterson/E+; Monty Rakusen/Cultura; Trevor Williams/DigitalVision; Image Source; **U4:** Visions of our Land/Photolibrary; RosLol/Moment; Hill Street Studios LLC/DigitalVision; **U5:** Hero Images; pixelfit/E+; Paul Bradbury/OJO Images; **U6:** vgajic/E+; Caiaimage/Sam Edwards; Tim Robberts/Taxi; **U7:** Luca Sage/Taxi; Ridofranz/iStock/Getty Images Plus; **U8:** Pierre-Yves Babelon/Moment; Johner Images; Kai-Otto Melau/Getty Images Sport; **U9:** LongHa2006/E+; Colin Hawkins/The Image Bank; Astrakan Images/Cultura; **U10:** Elena Odareeva/iStock Editorial/Getty Images Plus; Ashley Cooper/Corbis NX; SolStock/E+; Tuayai/iStock/Getty Images Plus; Westend61; **U13:** Manchan/DigitalVision; ranplett/E+; ianmcdonnell/E+; Alfredo Maiquez/Lonely Planet Images; **U14:** Nick Daly/Cultura; Vladimir Vladimirov/E+; Caiaimage/Chris Ryan/OJO+.

The following images are sourced from other sources/libraries

U2: Serhii Bobyk/Alamy Stock Photo.

Front cover photography by Supawat Punnanon/EyeEm; Patrick Foto; fStop Images-Caspar Benson.

Illustrations
Chris Chalik

Animations
Grammar animation video production by QBS Learnings. Voiceover by Dan Strauss.

Audio
Produced by Ian Harker and recorded at The SoundHouse Studios, London.
Reading text audio produced by Dan Strauss.

Page make up
Blooberry Design